Dark Psychology and Manipulation Techniques

How Learn to Read Body Language, Subconscious Mind, The Art of Persuasion, Secrets of Emotional Intelligence and NLP

ALBERT DANZELL

Page intentionally left blank

Table of Content

INTRODUCTION

The personality of human beings is a mind-blowing wellspring of activity and its novel for every individual we ordinarily meet in our life anyway. In the end, it's the same. This book explained it incredibly that psychological factors are not generally settled upon by everybody. And analysts have found that the culprits routinely experience the evil impacts of mental disorder or horrible accident in their lives that have caused them to become what their Personality is. It might be an explanation for their criminal act or why they hurt others, and this book is useful, supportive, and fascinating for all the individuals who need to think about how to analyze people by body language and behaviors and also learn about persuasion and dark psychology.

WHAT IS DARK PSYCHOLOGY?

Dark Psychology 101

Dark Psychology is the phenomenon by which individuals use strategies of inspiration, influence, control, and intimidation to get what they need. Dark Psychology is the examination of the human conditions to check how they get motivated and move after others and thus commits different criminal activities. All of the humankind can potentially victimize other people. While many limits or suppress this tendency, some follow up on these impulses.

Those thoughts, emotions, perceptions, and subjective processing systems are discussed in Dark Psychology that leads to savage conduct that is contradictory to present understandings of human behavior. Dark Psychology says that 99.99% of the time there is a purpose behind criminal acts and harsh modes. Dark Psychology hypothesizes there is an area inside the human mind that empowers a few people to submit dreadful acts without reason.

Dark Psychology says that all humanity can execute the pernicious plan towards others extending from being obtrusive and changeable states to pure psychopathic behavior with no durable rationality. This is known as the Dark Continuum.

Relieving factors that enable individuals to attract towards someone else and move towards the Dark Singularity, and where an individual's hurtful activities fall on the Dark Continuum, is the thing that Dark Psychology calls Dark Factor. A concise introduction to these ideas is discussed below. Dull Psychology discusses every aspect that makes our builds up our evil and dark side.

All humans are made with some of the darker sides inside them. No one can claim that he or she is pure of any evil side. Some people think of this side as criminal, immoral, and pathological. The fact is some tend to show there darker side while some do not have that caliber.

Dark Psychology presents a third philosophical development that sees these practices not quite the same as religious dogmas and contemporary sociology hypotheses.

Dark Psychology suggests that some individuals commit these acts, and they do not do because of power, cash, sex, or some other known reason. They commit these awful acts without an objective. Some people damage and harm others for satisfying themselves. Dark psychology tends to reside itself where someone hurt others without any clarification, objective, and cause.

Dark Psychology claims that we all have an innate ability to copy the behaviors of others. This ability precedes our emotions, thoughts, and perceptions. We have our emotions and feelings so we act rudely in one or another. We all have innate thinking of hurting others without any cause and being unkind to others.

In reality, we perceive ourselves as a kind and humble creature. We all have such emotions and thoughts but sometimes we are not ready to accept them. Dark Psychology presents some individuals who have these similar ideas, emotions, and perceptions, and they don't hesitate and pursue their plans. The main difference is some action on their projects, but others have those feelings for a short interval of time, and they disappear after that, leaving no intent of doing such a thing.

The part that triggers our predatory behavior is analyzed in the phenomenon of Dark Psychology. Lack of apparent rational impulse, wholeness, loss of predictability, and perception are remarkable characteristics of the behavioral. Dark Psychology understands this given human condition is modified or expansion of evolution. First, we need to think that we evolved from some animals and we are the best of all animals. Now assume that being best beings do not make us detached from our animal senses and predatory nature.

Considering it right if you contribute to evolution, then you think that all manners and behaviors relate to three primary instincts. Sex, aggression, and intelligence are the three fundamental human drives. Survival of the fittest and changing of the characters are key principles of the evolution.

The thing that makes us best among all is our control over our thinking and perceptions. Universally males fight till their death with immense power. This is the ritual of human societies. All actions, violence, and brutality explain a certain evolution.

We tend to see that while animals hunting, they often chase and kill the weakest of the crowd. The purpose of this action is to lessen the probability of their death. The animal world behaves in that manner. In this study of dark psychology, we will learn about the application of it on the species present on earth. Dark Psychology discusses that portion of the human psyche or general human condition that permits for the predatory behavior.

The great writers have tried their best to discuss this phenomenon. There are only humans that can cause harm to others without any cause or purpose. Dark Psychology believes there is a part of the human, which feeds vicious and wicked behaviors.

According to Dark Psychology, the dark side of humans is unpredictable. Some people torture, rape, murder, and violate without any cause or purpose. Dark Psychology talks to these activities of a man as a predator hunting prey without any reason. We humans are strangely dangerous to ourselves and even to other living creatures.

The more reader can imagine Dark Psychology, the better set up they become to decrease their odds of exploitation by human predators. Before continuing, it is important to have an awareness of Dark Psychology.

The following are six principles essential to understanding the Dark Psychology:

1. Dark Psychology is a general part of the human condition and has its impact from the beginning. All societies, social orders, and the individuals who live in them keep up this aspect of human health. The most kindhearted individuals known have this field of evil; however, they never followed it and have lower frequencies of rough ideas and emotions.

2. Dark Psychology is the examination of the human condition as it correlates with people groups' thoughts, emotions, and perceptions identified with this natural potential to hurt others without any cause. Given that all manner is purposive and goal-oriented, Dark Psychology suggests that lesser the person stay in the "dark hole" of evilness, the fewer chances there are for their purpose of inspiration.

3. There are a lot of historical instances where we can see unusual and dangerous activities. Currently, we can characterize a psychopath as a predator without regrets. Dark Psychology says that there is a continuum of seriousness extending from ideas and emotions of destruction to extreme exploitation without reason.

4. Dark psychology is considered as a wide scope of brutality. An honest description would analyze Ted Bundy and Jeffrey Dahmer. Both were extreme mental cases and horrifying in their activities. The thing that matters is Dahmer committed his murders for his odd requirement for friendship while Ted Bundy killed, out of pure psychopathic evilness. Both are higher on the Dark Continuum, yet one, Jeffrey Dahmer, can be better comprehended as he wanted to be loved.

5. Dark Psychology presumes all individuals have a potential for cruelty. This potential is inborn in all people, and different inner and outside components increase the likelihood of this possibility to show uncertainly. These practices are ruthless and occur occasionally. Dark Psychology is exclusively a human phenomenon and shared by no other living being. Violence and brutality may exist in other living beings, yet humans are the main kinds that can do without reason.

6. A comprehension of the unknown triggers of Dark Psychology would better empower society to perceive, analyze, and reduce the danger in its impact. Learning the ideas of Dark Psychology tells about its advantages as well. Besides, knowing the fundamentals of Dark Psychology accommodates our unique developmental reason for attempting to stay.

We were likely to teach others by expanding their awareness, making a change in their existence to improve things, and inspiring them to instruct others to try to figure out how to reduce the possibility of being the victim of these evil forces and how dark psychology help with this.

We all have our dark sides being the part of the human condition, yet not known lately. As this author has recently mentioned, Dark Psychology incorporates all types of brutal and violent behaviors.

This writer tries to look at Dark Psychology's starting point and nature to see how the healthy, intelligent individual can end up in the news, having an outrage behavior nobody could have expected. It is astonishing how people with good mental health might take an interest in, or permit such violence.

Great outrages are clear from history. There are enormous examples including destruction happened during World War II. As represented above, Dark Psychology is actual and alive, which requires a genuine discussion. As you keep on investigating the principles and establishment of Dark Psychology, a psychological structure of understanding will gradually create.

Dark Continuum

The Dark Continuum is a significant component to understand the dark section of humanity. The Dark Continuum is a hypothetical logical line or concentric circles that all corrupt criminals and sadist behavior lie. The Dark Continuum incorporates thoughts, emotions, observations, and activities experienced or potentially dedicated by people. The continuum ranges from purposeful to purposeless.

Mental appearances of Dark Psychology lie to one side of the continuum and they are as harmful as physical acts. The Dark Continuum isn't a scale of seriousness but ranges from poor to more terrible. When this author further grows his theory of the Dark Continuum, you will have a reasonable represented line describing all types of Dark Psychology running from purposeful to purposeless.

Dark Factor

The Dark Factor is characterized as the part that is there in our personality as a core part of the human condition. This idea is very conceptual that it is difficult to understand in words. As per an online dictionary, a factor is whatever contributes causally to an outcome, i.e., various elements determined the result. This author will try to extrapolate for you in a consistent tone how Dark Factor takes after a condition.

The Dark Factor is an exact condition, however, a hypothetical one. The Dark Factor is something a person encounters, which builds the possibility of engaging in violent conduct.

Even though exploration has proposed that youngsters who experience childhood in an abusive family become abusers themselves, this doesn't mean every mishandled kid develops to become violent. It is just a single aspect of a large number of experiences and conditions that add to the Dark Factor.

The quantity of components that are associated with the Dark Factor condition is enormous. It isn't the number of parts making Dark Factor outrageous. It is the effect that encounters an individual's emotional processing that makes the Dark Factor dangerous. A portion of these aspects incorporates hereditary qualities, relational characteristics, psychological insight, peer acceptance, sensitive treatment, and developmental accomplishments and experiences.

ADVANTAGES OF DARK PSYCHOLOGY

The dark psychology comes with advantages and disadvantages together. These are the two sides of the same coin. There is nothing in the world that comes out only with advantages. The same goes for the disadvantages that there is nothing in the world that only comes with disadvantages. It is always good and bad in the situation. The same goes for the dark psychology that there are some advantages and disadvantages to it. That is discussed below:

ADVANTAGES OF DARK PSYCHOLOGY

THERE IS NO MORE FEAR: People have a side of themselves that they fear. They don't want it to come in front of anybody. People take their dark side as a weakness because they fear the outcomes. Sometimes they also feel that it might overpower their personality. That's why they have issues of trust in themselves. As a result, they put themselves down a lot of time.

The Dark Side Is Not that dark as one thinks. It helps people to explore their weaknesses and the dark side of their personality. Once they get the hold of a dark side, they don't fear anything. Then, there is no more desire of approval seeking. Once it is out in front of the world, nothing is stopping you from achieving anything.

THEY ARE GOOD CONVINCERS: The Darker psychology side is very good at manipulating. They need to be great convincers. They need to know where to trigger a person and how to do it. Sometimes people standing for election in school and high school or general elections need to be great at convincing to get the votes. People whose dark side is a little more superior they can use a plus point and convince people to vote for them. It helps them achieve what they want but not in a bad manner until they are not destroying anybody. Sometimes fighting for their position turns out to be fine if they are doing it in a boundary. It gives people good convincing powers.

IT HELPS THEM TAKE RISK: there is nothing wrong with taking the risk if it is not having any bad result. a lot of people don't do a lot of things that they want to just because they are scared of the outcome especially when it comes to having fun. They experience everything in life, so the advantages of dark psychology are that since they don't say anything, they overcome their fear easily, and they probably live life to its fullest. It takes everything to do the following at the right moment, so sometimes their impulsiveness helps them have more fun as compared to the people who keep on thinking about the outcomes.

IT MAKES THEM GROW: the self-focus is not bad until it is not having any serious issue. Self-focus is very important for personal growth and personal maturity. Sometimes it helps people to focus on themselves completely and have them understand what they want in life to grow and to be a better person. It is something that helps a person to be a better person.

IT BRINGS OUT ENTHUSIASM: People with the opposite side of it are known as narcissists, and they are great at selling themselves. Similarly, they are great enthusiastic people because they try to be happier in situations that bring out the best results in the end.

ENTHUSIASM: you need to be full of energy ball for your ambitions. Enthusiasm for work is important for people. Great enthusiastic people know what they have to do in certain situations, so they are good people to work within a group.

THEY ARE VERY PRECISE: One of the dark psychology personality characteristics is that these people are very precise and careful. They always want to achieve much better than them. They are always looking out to work better and nice to make everything better. They are also known as perfectionists, so the probability of them making mistakes is very low. They are always trying to do something better, something that could be more appealing.

This type of person is great when it comes to achieving goals because they know what they want. They are so precious in doing everything, and it helps them succeed in life.

DISADVANTAGES OF DARK PSYCHOLOGY

THEY BECOME PARANOID: it undermines people in stressful circumstances and makes a person paranoid. Dark psychology mainly refers to the Dark Side, which causes a person to feel threatened in a lot of ways. They always keep on thinking that people are planning or working against them even though there is no truthfulness. They keep on making situations in their head that don't exist in the First Place. It happens a lot of time to a person, and sometimes people are also aware of the fact that it does not have any real basis, but still, they cannot stop themselves from feeling the fear. It can get more severe and sometimes turns out to be a mental health condition, but the darker side of the person just makes up something that whatever is happening has the motive against them, or it is a threat to them. The feeling that there is something that is actively trying to harm them when there is no search proves.

Even if something is happening in reality and it is happening in a positive and better way, some people think that there is something in it that is not right. They bring out the negative and positive aspects together, and later it costs them.

It is the dark psychology of the person at the darker side of the person who is suppressing the positive side, and no matter how much a person wants to stop, they can't stop. They keep on building situations and thoughts. Time to time, it is not linked to anything. It is a waste. It doesn't have any benefits.

THEY TURN INTO A HARMFUL MANIPULATOR: one of the things about dark psychology is that the people are great manipulators. Two different things are convincing, and manipulation is two different things convincing is a good trait, whereas manipulative people are the masters of deception.

Manipulative people are not interested in any other benefits of any other damages. They only want to gain control, and they want people to be unwillingly supportive in their plans. They have a lot of manipulative traits to trigger people. Whatever they say is hardly recognizable, it confuses a person to this extent that makes a person feel that they are crazy. They alter the truth in such a way, and they think lying would serve them in the end.

THEY PLAY THE VICTIM ROLE: people having a Dark Side or dark psychology and good in manipulating. they tend to play victim even if they are guilty in the situation would make the other person feel that everything that happens was their fault where they are not responsible. for manipulating and making situations in such a way that they turn into a victim. They would go to any extent to attest that they have nothing to do with the situation. They are really in that zone no matter what happens.

They are so good with the alteration of words that nobody even questions them in the situation. They are Masters when it comes to playing the victim role. They will play The Victim role to clear the situations. They will play The Victim card to get out of the situation. They won't care about how and what it costs to people out on the other side. They don't want to be jammed in a place that can be harmful to themselves. No matter if they are turning parasites on others. They only look for the good in themselves and no one else. They only want betterment in every situation and don't spare anyone when it comes to this.

THEY ARE NOT SINCERE: people having a Dark Side of The mind are really good manipulators. They are not sincere to anybody because they can put anyone down. Anybody who comes into their space is a threat to them. They love watching others going down, and they are willing to do anything bad.

They would lie in almost anywhere, and they would give the appearance of weakness because if it suits current needs, they will do whatever it would take. They would elaborate on situations in such a way that it would look so effective.

People having Dark Psychology perceive that it can harm anybody and their surroundings. Their life is so tamed that they are not loyal to anybody. They are not sincere. Sincerity is all the best thing a person can hold. They are not only lying to themselves, but they are also lying to every other person around them. They are not a truthful friend to be with. They are not faithful. They would do anything to make them dominating and greater no matter if the person they are harming is their blood relation. They don't see relationships are close enough. No matter what outcome it would bring later on.

IT OFTEN LOOKS LIKE THE ARE HYPOCRITE: they are not truthful to anybody and themselves. They keep on lying about situations. They are playing with other people's minds that they sometimes forget what they are doing and what reaction would lead to the end. They often show people what they are called like they are not their real selves. Being genuine is about being true to yourself and people surrounding you in every situation of life, which is why life has a set of events, and it seems to be the most trivial of occurrences. To approach life successfully, it is necessary to make the decisions that will divide the best that are the best outcome and at any given moment. A person has to be truthful and from to the best of their personalities and their need to be authentic. Every person is fake while going on the best things about our scenarios, and they think that it is necessary to be true to themselves. They know that they don't settle for less. They try to be a wannabe in these situations. They put on a mask on a face to hide the real personality because the dark triad of a mind that is overlapping is a genuine and truthful personality.

THEY CAN GET EXTREMELY AGGRESSIVE: they have difficulty in controlling their emotions no matter how much they try. They always come up with the reaction to situations, and anything that is caused because of their darker side damages their professional reputation. It is also a threat to their productivity, and eventually, they end up losing everything. In normal circumstances, it is very easy to maintain calm and composed, but sometimes when things get out of hand, and other impulsive reactions trigger people to get aggressive because they can't control the words in the actions and whatever they are doing. They feel that they have complete freedom of how they want to react to certain situations, but that is not the truth. The reaction should come up with responsibilities. They should know that no matter what they are doing, they should never cross the limits, but sometimes, because of their aggressive behavior towards people and things, they forget their boundaries.

That's why many people fear the darker side. They don't want to expose it to others. They can be so sweet that it leaves a person in trauma to understand what they want because they are following a person to them and insecurities and this also makes some very differences because of that they often lose the people they love. They can be very selfish and vicious whenever someone frames themselves from personal attacking and criticism, and there are dozens of pursuing ways of thinking that they can get whatever they want. They bully and threaten other people, and they won't let it stop until they destroy other people's mental peace.

THEY CAN PUT PEOPLE DOWN TO FEEL BETTER: when people are on the darker side of the mind of Psychology on the darker side of the mind, they don't care about what other people would think. What they think is only about everything that would benefit them would make them feel better that makes them stand out in certain situations.

They don't care that their actions will harm other people, and they are so much into the manipulation that when they talk with traits of their personality, it looks vicious. They would do anything to make other people feel down in front of them, which they do out of pleasure in doing so.

At that moment, they are in a subconscious state of mind. The feeling that it is nothing wrong until it is benefiting themselves; however, it is not only destroying their personality and is also destroying The Other person's life. They don't take charge of it either; that is why it is bad. A person on a darker side knows there if it comes out, it can harm people. It is very destructive to make other people fear a certain person to feel insecure and feel not safe around a certain person and in the end as a result of persons left lonely, and they don't have anybody else except regrets.

IT MAKES THEM ANTI SOCIAL: the state of mind is so wicked, and it makes the person antisocial. The antisocial person is not a person who hates to go out and mingle with people because being an introvert and being an antisocial person are two different things. When a person says that they are antisocial, they are mistakenly known as the people who don't like to be around others, whereas in this context, it is the opposite of pro-social. this is that the anti-social person is very actively harmful towards other than if they are present in certain situations. They can cause harm to the person. They are so self-centered on the surface that they are a threat to others, and they lack empathy, and it is also combined with impulsiveness. The mix of impulsiveness and lack of empathy makes them harmful to others because they would do what they want to do at the moment. They would not think twice before doing so.

This is one of the most Dark Side of The Dark psychology that is better if it doesn't come out. That is why they set the people who are going through this need therapy because otherwise, they can be a threat to themselves and society. When they do this, they don't think, and they don't have any motive sometimes too because they think that it is quite normal; however, harming other people is not normal especially when you find comfort in doing so; however, people might think that these types of people are better if they stay at home; however, it was just causing them and provoke them to harm themselves so they should get therapies to help themselves and others in a better manner.

THEY HAVE NO SET OF BOUNDARIES: every person has certain measures in their life. They have certain limitations, and they know that they can't cross the limitations because if they do, it will cause harm to them and others.

They don't want to be a Rebel for discomfort for people around them but when people are so manipulative, and they can easily hypnotize others, and there in the dark psychology side they have no boundaries because in their eyes whatever they are doing is right and they don't take responsibility for every action. They don't think of a backup plan; they don't think of what it can cause and why and what can cause other people because, at that moment, if they are thinking of it, that if they want to do certain things, they will do it.

They would do anything to achieve their goals whether it would take intimidation, Persuasion, force, or seduction whatever it would take they would do it just because they think that there are no boundaries if they won't do a certain activity they want to achieve a certain goal which is very wrong which might be very thrilling and exciting for them because people with the dark psychology of Mind need a lot of thrill in their life because they think that they have a lot of higher self-esteem than others.

However, it is a quality of a coward who doesn't set boundaries of their actions, and sometimes they are very successful in doing so, but then it leads to difficulties when there are long-standing relationships. They have very little regard for what others would feel in this way.

THEY ARE SELF CENTERED: Self-centered is also known as narcissism and when a person wants to be the center of attention. They would do anything to gain attention and make sure that they are the star of everything. They will take any opportunity to do something big of themselves to others that is so in hands and so fake. They don't care about how it would generally affect a place or a certain group of people. They don't like to be ignored because they are so much into themselves that the fact that they might lose the attention they want. They may not be a center of attention somewhere whatever they are doing over there. They get so compulsive about their behavior and so upset about themselves that nearly is destroying everything.

There is a chance that everything around them starts to fade away, and when people try showing them their places, they are not good at taking it. They don't like criticism when exposed to them because, according to them, they feel like their perfectionist and nothing can go wrong.

THEY ARE NOT RESPONSIBLE: they avoid responsibilities for their own. They find out, and then after a matter happens, they blame others for the cause. it's not that they don't understand what the responsibility is they do, but they just don't want to take the whole control, and they don't think that there is anything wrong if they are not taking charge or responsibility of their actions or any other thing. In general, they would force others to take the responsibilities, and they would not give any regards of their responsibilities. They would take the responsibility so they can satisfy their own needs and they turn into a parasite and host it to other people.

Then they leave no room for other people to fulfill their responsibilities because they are so busy making other to do so. They are confined in making themselves happy.

THEY LACK UNDERSTANDING: people crowd themselves in a space that is physically, emotionally, and spiritually of no concern to them. They highly care about what they want instead of thinking that they are turning into a parasite in human form and the natural world; this is said to be acceptable in a relationship. However, feeding of at someone's expense and mental peace is very exhausting and weakening and is also demeaning. Not only are they not taking charge of themselves, but they are also destroying the other person in every possible way, so nobody wants a parasite in their life no matter how hard it is to get rid of it. People can't get rid of it, so these types of people are so vulnerable that people find it easier to leave them because they are so toxic that nobody wants to be around them.

THEY PREY ON CONSCIENTIOUS: they prey on personal sensibilities and emotional sensitivity because they know that they have a great chance of getting somebody into a relationship by manipulating them and making them feel like they are very kind and very caring. They are trained in such a way, and that causes other people to get into the governors and kindness first and then slowly for how wonderful they are but after the time passes they face and judge that these qualities minimize because the person feels is that they are only being used of service by somebody because they don't care about anything. they just only care about what is being given to them, and their criteria are always given and never give and take. This personality is very self-centered, and they are very Emotionless.

WHAT IS NLP? 5 NLP TECHNIQUES THAT WILL TRANSFORM YOUR LIFE

Five NLP techniques can help you to figure out a better and bright future. These five key points can also help you to change your behavior.

Top 5 NLP Techniques That Will Transform Your Life:

1. Dissociation

Have you ever trapped in a certain situation where you feel so bad? There are chances that you have gone through some experience that has brought you down. There is also a chance that you get into such a situation where you need to speak publically. Maybe you get shy when you want to approach that "special someone" you've had your eye on. When you feel sadness, nervousness, and shyness, NLP techniques help you the most.

First of all, you need to figure out the feeling from which you want to get rid of. Then you need to think that you can float out from your body that means you can escape from your intense feelings. You can note that your feeling can change dramatically.

2. Content Reframing

You need to go with this technique when you are in a helpless or negative situation. You can change your perspective and can overcome your negative situation with the help of reframing.

For example, let's say that your relationship ends. This example may seem irritating but let us reframe it. Now, you need to think what are the possible advantages of being single? You can think that you are free to do anything. Now no one can rule over you and you have the potential to commit to other relationships. From this relationship, you might have learned a lot of lessons that have made you a better person now.

These are all examples of reframing a situation. By reframing the meaning of the breakup, you give yourself a different experience of it.

In expected situations, it is very natural that you get fear bout you have to drag your attention. You need to divert your focus so that you can be responsible and decisive.

3. Anchoring Yourself

Anchoring originates with Russian scientist Ivan Pavlov who experimented with dogs by ringing a bell repeatedly while the dogs were eating. After repeated rings of the bell, he found he could get the dogs to salivate by ringing the bell anytime, even if there was no food present.

This created a conditioned response through the neurological association between the bell and the behavior of salivating.

You can associate any desired positive emotional response with a particular phrase or sensation by anchoring yourself. When you choose a positive emotion or thought and deliberately connect it to a simple gesture, you can trigger this anchor any time you're feeling low, and your feelings will immediately change.

Identify what you want to feel (e.g. confidence, happiness, calmness, etc.)

Besides you need to decide how and where you will place an anchor. You can place it by pulling your earlobe, touching your knuckle, or pressing a fingernail. Through this physical touch, you can trigger a positive feeling according to your will.

Try to mentally go into the past and suppose that can float into your body. Look through your eyes and try to relive that memory. You need to adjust your body according to the state.

See what you saw, hear what you heard, and feel the feeling as you remember that memory. You will begin to feel that state. This is similar to telling a friend a funny story from the past, and as you "get into" the story, you start to laugh again, because of you "associate" to the story and "relive" it. Now as you have gone to the past touch your that body part that you have chosen. As you release the touch the same moment the emotional state peaks and begins to wear off.

In this order, a neurological stimulus-response will be triggered and the state whenever you make that touch again. If you want to feel that state then you need to that body part again.

4. Getting Other People to Like You (Rapport)

This is an easy set of NLP techniques, but they have the power to help you get along with virtually anyone. There are lots of ways to build rapport with another person. NLP gives you one of the quickest and effective ways.

In this technique, another person's body language, tone of voice, and words are subtly mirrored.

In this way the brain of a person fires off "mirror neurons," and thus pleasure is sensed in the brain. This makes people feel a sense of liking for anyone mirroring them.

The technique is simple: you need to imitate the way of sitting, head-tilting, or smile. You need to mirror the expressions of other people. You can copy the voice tone of others. Moreover, it is very important to copy expressions calmly and naturally.

5. Influence and Persuasion

Where NLP techniques help to eliminate negative emotions, limiting beliefs, bad habits, conflict, and more it also helps to influence and persuade others at the same time. Milton H. Erickson is one of the highly recognized mentors. Erickson was a psychiatrist who also studied the subconscious mind through hypnotherapy.

He proposed a way of talking to the subconscious minds without hypnosis. He could hypnotize the people anytime and anywhere. This Ericksonian method of hypnosis became known as "Conversational Hypnosis."

This is a very powerful tool to help other people overcome fears, limiting beliefs, conflict, and more without their conscious awareness. This is especially useful when getting across to people who might otherwise be resistant if they know.

DARK PSYCHOLOGY AND ANALYZING PEOPLE

When you are learning to analyze people, the responsibility is to understand people, what they state, yet what their identity is. Understanding verbal and nonverbal signals, you need to see past their veils into the genuine person. Reason alone won't disclose to you the entire story about them. You should surrender on other essential data so you can figure out how to read the significant non-verbal natural signs that individuals speak.

To do this, you should likewise be eager to give up any previously established capabilities, or psychological weight, for example, old feelings of hatred or personality conflicts that prevent you from seeing somebody. The key is to stay objective and get data impartially without damaging it.

Regardless you're reading your leader, colleague, or assistant to comprehend individuals precisely; you should give up options. A few dividers must descend. As great the vision may be, you must be happy to abandon old, restricting thoughts. Individuals who read others well are prepared to understand the hidden. They've figured out how to use their "super-senses" to look farther than where you are.

ANALYZING PEOPLE'S BEHAVIOR AND READING BODY LANGUAGE

One of the major components of pulling off Dark Psychology's tactics of persuasion and manipulation is to *understand* the person that you want to manipulate by analyzing their behavior. In other words, you should be able to read their body language. According to science, about 20% of communication between people is through spoken words. What about the other 80% then? That is all body language.

What *is* body language? It is the frequency that allows you to read other people like an open book. Google defines body language as 'the conscious and unconscious movements and postures by which attitudes and feelings are communicated.' Though this definition caters to both conscious and unconscious, it is safe to say that most people are *not consciously aware* of their behaviors. Without realizing it, every person on this planet is broadcasting a signal.

If you can learn to tune into that signal's frequency and pay attention to tiny details put forth, not only can you understand the other person and their behaviors, but also manipulate them if you wish. If you learn how to analyze each person's signal, besides being able to see what is unseen by most (even the person themselves), you will be able to understand what exactly it is that they are thinking. You will be able to read minds, and then, if you want, even change them. That is exactly how people use Dark Psychology. Now the question is how do you analyze people's behavior and read minds? I have already mentioned that you have to tap into some frequency, in other words, see their movements and postures, and, as some professional psychologists put it, their "tells," but how does it all add up together? Well, it has already been established that the mind and the body are mirrors of each other, and are directly linked. Whatever someone is thinking or feeling, their body will broadcast it one way or another. All you have to do is interlink your intuition with your intellectual capacity, i.e., your comprehension.

An FBI agent from America, when interviewed, said that one does not have to be a top-notch interrogator to be able to figure out what it is that is going inside someone's head, and she even shared her top nine secrets into reading people:

1. Figure out the baseline personality;
2. Look for deviations from that baseline;
3. Notice clusters of behavioral aberrations;
4. Compare the deviations from the baseline;
5. Understand whether or not actions are reciprocated;
6. Identify the strong voice;
7. Observe people's walk;
8. Recognize the kind of words they use to describe actions; and
9. Understand what their personality clues are.

Now, let's get into the specifics of these. Every day, people display some random odd behaviors. When these behaviors come to light, you realize that 'yes, something is off,' but you do not know what exactly or why.

The realization is your intuition telling you that something weird is happening, the 'gut feeling' you have now and then. Comprehension comes into play when you want to figure out what and why your intuition is telling you so. Let us take an example. There is a boy who snuck out of his house one night to go to a party with his friends. The very next morning, his mother asks him why he hadn't slept, considering she heard a little bit of commotion at night when she woke up to pray. Around that time, the boy was sneaking back into the house after the party, but of course, he could not tell his mother that. So, he told her that he was up studying all night for a test. While telling this lie, the boy scratched his head. At face value, this behavior might just seem like the boy has an itch, but depending on the context of this situation, it can also show that the boy is dishonest; that is, he is trying to deceive his mother. It is because of these small gestures that parents can expertly figure out when you are lying to them. They know your Baseline Behavior.

Baseline Behavior is the one that is steady in form and the standard. This makes it easier to spot any tiny changes in the way you act or respond. So, if you ever deviate from your baseline behavior, their intuition tells them that something is not right, and hence they realize that you are lying. This is not just true for finding out when someone is lying, but for multiple other scenarios as well, for example, a girl raises her left eyebrow constantly when she is feeling angry, or a boy sniffs his nose often when he is feeling nervous. From the face value, it may look like the boy has gotten a cold or runny nose, but the truth is that this tiny gesture depicts that the boy is nervous.

So, one way to read body language is to constantly observe someone until you figure out how they behave under different conditions. Another way to understand people's behaviors in a situation, or people themselves, is through their tone of voice. When you come across a group of people, notice the one with the strongest voice.

That person has the personality of a strong person. Some voices will be soft, some will be loud, but only one will be strong and firm as compared to the other voices. It is important to distinguish between the strongest voice and loudest voice. Just because someone is loud, does not mean they are the leader of the group. The leader can have a soft-spoken voice, but it would be stern, and it would project confidence. The voice tone of someone greatly determines what kind of personality they are and whether or not they can be easily manipulated. Someone with a strong voice means that they have an Active Personality that is strong-willed and of strong character, will the opposite will be true for someone with a Passive Personality.

However, to truly understand someone's body language, only focusing on one aspect is not enough. You must look into more than just one sign, so other than focusing on their tone of voice; you can also try to analyze someone through their walking style. Every person has a different walking style, and that style reflects their personality more than one realizes.

Of course, there are always exceptions to these assumptions, but in the majority of the cases, a person with a strong walk has a strong personality, and that is another feature that will help you realize whether this is someone who can be easily coerced and persuaded or not. A strong walk is one where the person takes moderate and confident strides, with each step seeming to be meaningful, making it seem as though they have somewhere important to be. People with weak personalities either take short shuffled and aimless steps, showing a sense of constant confusion in their mind, or they will take extra-long and fast strides, making it seem as though they are very rushed and in a hurry, implying an anxious mind. Besides the tone of voice and walking style, the words someone chooses to speak can quite possibly also help you read their body language. This is the most obvious form and over time you can also grasp what words you should use to get someone to do what you want. Confident words show a confident personality, and the opposite would be true if the person using statements like 'I guess,' or 'I don't know.'

This is because these words make it seem like the person does not have control over their life, and are always beating around the bush rather than just being straightforward and concise. Such people are more prone to being a victim to dark psychological tactics, as they simply let things happen to them, rather than try to take control. Another example can be that of a regional manager, who in a meeting, states, "I decided to get things done." The word 'decided' shows that she did not just aimlessly make a decision, but rather put thought into it and knows how to take control of the situation.

Similarly, the way a person behaves is also dependent on what their birth order is. There are four categories: Oldest, Youngest, Middle, and Only Child. The oldest child will tend to form jealous rivalries when they start losing their parent's attention due to the younger one. This eventually causes them to develop a jealous and unconfident nature. The youngest competes for attention with the oldest, and always wants to get their way.

The youngest child's personality is also that of a risk-taker most of the time because they feel like they can whatever it is that they want. The middle child tends to become very arrogant because even at home, they receive the least amount of attention, so they try to take it out in other ways. Only children are more sensitive to criticism, and they also develop attention-seeking habits. By knowing what the person's birth order is, you can easily work around their specific personality traits to get what you want out of them.

Tuning in to the frequency of body language and basic human psychology will tell you so much about a person. To accurately use dark psychological methods, it is very important to understand people's behaviors.

THREE METHODS IN THE ART OF READING PEOPLE

The First Technique: Observe Body Language signs
Research has demonstrated that words represent just 7 percent of how we convey though our non-verbal communication (55 percent) and voice tone (30 percent) speak to the rest. Here, the surrender to concentrate on is abandoning a decent attempt to read non-verbal communication hints. Try not to get excessively exceptional or scientific.

Remain loose and free. Be agreeable, sit back, and watch.

1. Focus on Appearance
When reading, you must notice: Are they wearing a comfortable suit and polished shoes, dressed for progress, expressing desire? Pants and a T-shirt, showing solace with being relaxed?

A tight top with cleavage, an enticing decision? A pendant, for example, wearing a cross or Buddha showing spiritual values.

2. Observe Posture

When reading individuals' Posture, ask yourself: Do their head is high? Or, on the other hand, do they walk hesitantly or crawl, an indication of low confidence? Do they walk with a puffed-out chest, a sign of an egoistic personality?

3. Observe the Physical Movements

Inclining and distance—observe where individuals lean. For the most part, we attract those whom we like and get away from those whom we don't like.

This Posture of crossed arms and legs recommends prevention, indignity, or protectiveness. At the point when individuals fold their legs, they will, in general, point the toes of the top leg faces the person they are most close.

When individuals place their hands in their laps, pockets, or put them despite their great faith, it recommends that they are hiding something.

When individuals nibble or lick their lips or pick their fingernail skin, they are attempting to ease themselves under tension or in an awkward circumstance.

4. Read Facial Expression

Feelings can get scratched on our faces. Profound expression proposes stress or over-thinking. Crow's feet are the smile lines of delight. Pursed lips signal hatred, arrogance, or sharpness. A clasped jaw and teeth crushing are indications of stress.

The Second Technique: Listen to Your Intuition

You can tune into somebody past their non-verbal communication and words. Your gut feeling is not that what your head says. It is nonverbal data you see using pictures and has no logic. If you need to get somebody, what sums the most is who the individual is, not their external trappings.

Instinct lets you see farther than the undeniable to uncover a more fantastic story.

List of Intuitive Ideas

1. Consider your Gut feelings

Tune in to what your gut says, particularly during first meetings, an instinctive response that happens before you get an opportunity to think. It transfers whether you're calm or not. Ideas happen rapidly, a necessary reaction. They're your interior truth meter, moving if you can trust individuals.

2. Feel the goosebumps

Goosebumps are magnificent instinctive shivers that pass on that we reverberate with individuals who move or rouse us or are stating something that hits. Goosebumps additionally happen when you experience this feels familiar, an acceptance that you've known somebody previously. However, you've never met.

3. Focus on flashes of thought

In discussions, you may get an "ah-ha" about individuals who arrive instantly. Remain alert. Else, you may miss it. We will, in general, go onto the following idea so quickly, these essential parts of knowledge are lost.

4. Watch for intuitive sympathy

Once in a while, you can feel individuals' physical side effects and feelings in your body, which is a severe type of compassion. All in all, when understanding individuals, notice: "Does my back hurt when it didn't previously? Am I discouraged or upset after a routine gathering?" To decide whether this is empathy, get input.

The Third Technique: Sense Emotional Energy

Feelings are a shocking connection of our vitality, the "vibe" we emit. We register these with instinct. A few people feel great to associate with; they improve your state of mind and imperativeness.

Others are depleting; you intuitively need to escape. This "modest energy" can be felt inches or feet from the body. However, it's hidden. In Chinese medication, it's called chi, an essentialness that is fundamental to wellbeing.

Procedures to Read Emotional Energy

1. Observe People's Presence

That is the universal energy we radiate, not consistent with words or conduct. It's the passionate climate surrounding us like a downpour cloud or the sun. As you read individuals, notice: Do they have a friendly approach that draws in you? Or would you say you are getting the creeps, making you ease off?

2. Follow People's Eyes

Our eyes transmit fantastic energy. Similarly, as the cerebrum has an electromagnetic sign reaching out past the body, studies demonstrate that the eyes feel this as well.

Set aside some effort to watch individuals' eyes. It is very safe to say that they are mindful? Hot? Quiet? Mean? Irate? Likewise, decide: Is there somebody at home in their eyes, demonstrating a limit with regards to closeness? Or on the other hand, do they appear to be protected or stowing away?

3. Observe the Feel of a Handshake, Hug, and Touch

We share enthusiastic energy through physical contact, a lot of like an electrical flow. Ask yourself, does a handshake or a hug feel warm, pleasant, and certain? Or, on the other hand, do you need to pull back? Are individuals' hands are moist, showing tension. Or then again hesitate, recommending being reserved and shy?

4. Tune in for Tone of Voice and Laugh

The frequency and volume of our voice can educate much concerning our feelings. Sound frequencies make vibrations. When understanding individuals, notice how their manner of speaking influences you.

Ask yourself: Does their tone feel relieving? Or is it grating, rude, or whiny?

Subconscious language

The subconscious is perceived as the wellspring of creativity, instinct, motivation, internal knowing, interconnectedness, and spirituality. Inside this domain, reality moves and grows, making a grid that is more versatile and multi-dimensional than is seen by the conscious brain. When we get to spend time in the subconscious, we are discharged from the limits of our logical and rational mind. The messages we get from our fantasies and the primordial symbols, or the teaching from our ancestors, teach us about what is excellent, reliable, and sacred to every one of us. At the point when we regard these messages, we are following the way of our spirit's advancement.

These images and archetypes are essential components of the collective unconscious, the general intra-psychic organizing device inborn to people. It seems as though the crucial progressed data learned by previous eras is given to us as an easy route to our development. When something is found out related to human awareness, it isn't essential to learn it again. It is inborn, lasting forever, with being human.

The "endless language" of the unconscious lives inside us always served to offer hints and information, offers, and cues. Figuring out how to get to the subconscious and to ultimately use its abilities can assist us with seeing in another manner. Past our conscious brain and regular detect, the cover is lifted, uncovering a universe of boundless possibilities.

What is so penetrating here is that words are powerless to tell or pass on a message? The symbol, the authentic picture or design, moves on the whole idea, concept, or perfect without the utilization of words to describe it.

The thought is enormously powerful, for the way we "talk" to ourselves, our internal language, how we know what our identity is, doesn't originate from words, but instead from the constant source inside that understands what our identity is.

A short instructional exercise, if you don't have a clue about this as of now. The left hemisphere of the mind controls the vast majority of the neuromuscular and motor working on the right side. The right half controls the left side. However, there is a massive contrast concerning the quality and character of the hemisphere. The left side of the region is, to a great extent, involved with intelligent, analytical thinking as in verbal and numerical abilities. In contrast, the right side of the hemisphere is generally liable for direction in space, self-perception, recognition of appearances, and imaginative efforts.

The right side of the body or body-mind is related to the masculine and characteristics related to it are "self-assuredness, aggressiveness, and coercion." The left side is viewed as female, and attributes associated with it are "emotionality, lack of involvement, creative idea, and holistic expressions.

An interesting ongoing hypothesis recommends that a "holistic, synchronous, synthetic, and firm perspective on the world are the basic attributes of a female viewpoint; straight, consecutive, reductionist, and conceptual reasoning characterizes the masculine." Every individual has the full limit concerning both of these sets. In a perfect world, these should exist together similarly, with neither more significant nor stable than the other.

Leonard Shlain, in The Alphabet Versus the Goddess, presents convincing evidence to propose that the appearance of the composed word, and afterward the letters in order, moved the outlook of recently skilled societies.

Word and pictures are "correlative opposites" that they are intended to exist together on equal balance. However, while preliterate societies lifted everything feminine, the progress toward the written word supported the masculine and male-controlled culture rose and, in the long run, dominated.

While this hypothesis is relatively incredible and may clarify a considerable amount about how things found a workable pace way they are, that is not the point. What is frequently significant is the possibility that the subconscious uses imagery and symbolism to communicate, and the damaging of the idea for the word may have harmed how we think as humanity. This may clarify the failure of holistic expression so related to the right cerebrum. It has been recommended that TV, film, and the Internet might be reintroducing the images that represent elevated awareness and holistic expression. We can hope that is real.

HUMAN INTERACTION

Human is a social animal. We desire contact with others for help, prosperity, and entertainment. However, as our ways of life become permanently moving and dependent on advanced instruments, these honest interactions are under risk. Nothing compares to living in whole communities and investing real physical time with our loved ones.

For what reason is human interaction is significant?

For a specific thing, it is significant for our emotional wellbeing. Human contact causes life changes as separation, return, and moving house. Realizing that others value us is a significant subconscious factor in helping us to overlook the negative parts of our lives, and thinking all the more emphatically about our condition.

There is convincing evidence to recommend human contact is likewise fundamental for our physical wellbeing as well. In a report, 2010 t in The Journal of Health and wellness and Social Behavior, Debra Umberson and Jennifer Karas Montez, humanism analysts at the University of Texas at Austin, referred to confirm connecting a low quality or quantity of social ties with a large group of conditions, including the advancement and cardiovascular disease, repeat coronary episodes, immune system issue, hypertension, a cancerous growth, and slow healing process.

Now and again, a hearing issue may prompt trouble sharing, ultimately in discussions pounding away, home, and in social events. This may aid withdrawing from events that demonstrate excessively inquiring. Be that as it may, in these conditions, to stay away from scenes of withdrawal and sadness, human interaction is considered significant.

Four different ways to improve the nature of your human connections:

1. Use technology to encourage, not replace, social interaction: Whatsapp and Facetime are phenomenal applications; however, a relationship dependent on electronic variations is one destined to fail. Use technology to encourage shared experiences as a significant aspect of your family life.

2. Organize human interaction in both your professional and private life. Make time routinely in your schedule for gatherings yet additionally for casual meals and espressos. It is regularly at these loose and casual meet-ups where we learn with the most.

3. Connect with individuals who make you happy. Acknowledge you will never get on with everybody, and direct interaction with those individuals who bring you happiness.

4. Live in an instant network, or assemble your own. Offer assistance and support to the individuals who need it. No one can tell when you will require help consequently. Leave the schedule and be available to immediate interactions.

Body Language.

 Body Language refers to the nonverbal signs that we use to convey. A significant part of communication is dependent upon these non-verbal signs. From our outer appearances to our body developments, the things we don't state can convey a lot of information.

It is proposed that body Language may represent 60 percent to 65 percent of all communication. Understanding Body Language is significant. However, it is additionally fundamental to focus on different clues, for example, context. As a rule, you should take a look at signals as a group instead of concentrating on a single activity.

Interpretation of Body Language

1 Facial expressions

Ponder how much an individual can convey with only facial expression. A smile can show permission or joy. A frown can signal anxiety or despair. In many cases, our facial expression may uncover our actual emotions about a specific event. While you state that you are feeling fine, the look of your face may tell individuals in any case.

Only a couple of examples of emotions that can be communicated using facial expressions include:

- Joy
- Pain
- Insult
- Shock
- disgust
- Dread
- Confusion
- Enthusiasm
- Desire
- Hatred

The face of an individual helps to decide the level of trust of that person. One investigation found that the most sincere facial expression included a slightly raising the eyebrows and a slight smile. This association, the experts recommended, passes on both happiness and confidence.

Facial expression is additionally among the universal types of body Language. The look used to convey dread, anger, distress, and content are similar all over the world.

Expert Paul Ekman has discovered help for the universality of a variety of facial expressions attached to specific feelings, including delight, anger, dread, shock, and sadness.

Research even proposes that we make decisions about individuals' intelligence, dependent on their faces and expressions. One examination found that people who had a narrow face look and prominent noses were bound to be seen as intelligent.

Individuals with smiling, happy expression were likewise determined as being more intelligent than those with angry emotions.

The Eyes

The eyes are as often as possible referred to as the "windows to the spirit." Since they can uncover a lot about what an individual is feeling or thinking.

As you communicate with someone else, the observance of the listener's eye is a very unique part of communication.

When assessing Body Language, focus on the eye signals:

Eye stare: When an individual looks straightforwardly at you while having a discussion, it demonstrates that they are interested and focusing. However, you can negotiate with a keen eye to eye connection. Turning away may show that the individual is distracted, awkward, or trying to hide their genuine feelings.

Blinking: Blinking is regular but you need to check whether an individual is blinking regularly or little. Individual blinks regularly when they are feeling upset or awkward. Rare Blinking may demonstrate that an individual is purposefully attempting to control their eye movements. For instance, a poker player may Blink less as often as possible since he is deliberately trying to seem unexcited about the hand he was managed.

Pupil size: Pupil size can be an elementary nonverbal communication signal. While light levels in the surface control pupil dilation, here and there feelings can likewise cause little changes in pupil size. For instance, you may have heard the expression "bedroom eyes" used to represent the look somebody gives when they are attracted to someone else. Exceptionally dilated eyes, for instance, can demonstrate that an individual is intrigued or even aroused.

The Mouth

Mouth expressions and developments can likewise be basic in reading Body Language. For instance, biting on the base lip may show that the individual is facing feelings of stress, dread, or instability.

An individual can hide his or her anxiety and perceived as to be gracious while yawning or hacking. Smiling is maybe one of the best body Language signals. However, smiles can also be interpreted in many ways. A smile might be real, or it might be utilized to communicate false joy, joke, or even cynicism.

When assessing body Language, focus on the mouth and lip signals:

Pursed lips: Tightening the lips maybe a hint of dislike, objection, or doubt.

Lip Biting: People, some of the time, bite their lips when they are concerned, on point, or focused.

Covering the mouth: When individuals need to hide an enthusiastic response, they may cover their mouths to abstain from showing smirks or smiles.

Turned up or down: Individuals can shoe a lot of changes just by showing little indicator. An individual is said to be cherished or hopeful when the mouth is turned up. Then again, a somewhat down-turned mouth can be a hint of misery, anxiety, or even an inside and outfrown.

Gestures

Gestures can be the clear Body Language signals. Waving, pointing, and utilizing the fingers to show exponential sums are, for the most part, extraordinarily ordinary and abrupt gestures.

These examples are only a couple of natural gestures and their possible connections:

- A clench fisted hand can demonstrate anger in certain circumstances or solidarity in others.

- Thumbs up and down are frequently utilized as signals of approval and disapproval.
- The "ok" gestures, made by contacting together the thumb and forefinger around while broadening the other three fingers, can be utilized to signify "alright." In certain parts of Europe, however, a similar sign is used to suggest you are nothing. In some South American nations, the image is a low signal.
- The V sign, made by lifting the index and center finger and isolating them to make a V-shape, implies harmony or triumph in some nations. In the United Kingdom and Australia, the image when the back of the hand facing outward is very important.

The Arms and Legs

The arms and legs can likewise be valuable in passing on nonverbal information. Crossing the arms can show prevention and crossing legs from someone else may show hatred or inconvenience with that person.

Other hidden signals, for example, extending the open arms, might be an attempt to appear to be bigger or more directing while at the same time keeping the arms near the body might be an attempt to minimize himself withdraw attention.

At the point when you are assessing Body Language, focus on the part of the signs that the arms and legs may convey.

- Crossed arms may demonstrate that an individual feels careful, self-defensive, or shut off.

- Standing with hands set on the hips can be a sign that an individual is prepared and in charge, or it can likewise be an indication of aggressiveness.

- Clasping the hands behind the back may show that an individual is feeling exhausted, on end, or even enraged.

- Fast tapping fingers or squirming can be an indication that an individual is fatigued, anxious, or frustrated.

- Crossed legs can show that an individual is feeling stopped or needing protection.

Posture

How we carry our bodies can likewise play a significant part in Body Language. The term act referred to how we hold our bodies just as the general physical type of a person. Posture can convey an abundance of information about how an individual is feeling just as insights about Personality features, for example, regardless of whether an individual is trustworthy, open, or agreeable.

For instance, sitting upright shows that person is engaged where something is happening. Sitting with the body slouched forward, then again, can infer that the individual is exhausted or detached.

When you are reading Body Language, try focusing on the signs that an individual's Posture can send.

- Open Posture includes keeping the trunk of the body open and uncovered. This sort of Posture shows kind friendliness, clearness, and willingness.

- Closed Posture includes covering the trunk of the body frequently by slouching forward and keeping the arms and legs crossed. This kind of Posture can be a signal of an unfriendly vibe, disagreeableness, and anxiety.

Have you caught somebody referred to their requirement for personal space? Have you begun to feel awkward when somebody stands near you?

The term proxemics, authored by anthropologist Edward T. Corridor, referred to the distance between individuals as they communicate. Similarly, as body developments and facial expression can convey a lot of nonverbal data, so can this physical space between people.

Four degrees of social distance that happen in various circumstances:

Close range —6 to 18 inches: This degree of physical distance frequently shows a closer relationship or more prominent solace between people.

It usually happens during intimate contact, for example, hugging, murmuring, or contacting.

Personal distance—1.5 to 4 feet: Physical distance at that level happens typically between individuals who are relatives or dear companions. The closer the individuals can comfortably stand while communicating can be an indicator of the degree of closeness in their relationship.

Social Distance—4 to 12 feet: This degree of physical separation is regularly utilized with people who are colleagues. With somebody you know genuinely well, for example, a colleague you see a few times each week, you may feel great interfacing at a closer separation. In situations where you don't have the idea about the other individual well, for example, a postal conveyance driver you observe once per month, a distance of 10 to 12 feet may feel good.

Public Distance—12 to 25 feet: Physical distance at this level is regularly utilized in full daylight speaking situations. Talking before a class loaded with students or giving an introduction at work are excellent cases of such circumstances. It is critical to take note that the degree of individual distance that people need to feel great can fluctuate from culture to culture. One example is the distinction between individuals from Latin societies and those from North America. Individuals from Latin nations will, in general, feel progressively significant, standing more like each other as they cooperate while those from North America need increasingly close to home separation.

Understanding Body Language can go far toward helping you better speak with others and interpreting what others may be attempting to convey. While it might be enticing to end signs individually, it's imperative to take a look at these nonverbal signals corresponding to verbal communication, other nonverbal symbols, and the circumstance.

You can likewise concentrate on getting familiar with how to improve your nonverbal communication to turn out to be better at telling individuals what you are feeling—without saying a word.

What is Personality Type?

The possibility of a Personality "type" is genuinely far-reaching. Numerous individuals associate a "Type A" Personality with a progressively ordered, determined, competitive, and anxious individual, while a "Type B" Personality signals versatility, creativeness, and relaxed. However, there's little experimental help for the idea. It didn't rise out of psychology—two cardiologists made the idea as an approach to understand the association between stressed patients and the probability of developing coronary illness and hypertension.

Analysts who study Personality accept such typologies frequently are too shortsighted to even think about accounting for the numerous ways individuals differ in Personality.

Instead, there is a comprehensive logical accord around the Big Five. Every one of these critical qualities adds to one's Personality and is free of the others.

In appreciation, for the most part, staying stable over one's lifetime, they can likewise anticipate behavior in specific events or connect with life results. Great uprightness, for instance, is related to higher lifetime income.

VISUAL INTERACTION AND READING OTHER BEHAVIOR

When someone Closing their eyes

When someone closes his or her eyes while interacting with you. Then this symbolizes that they are trying their best to hide something from you and the outside world. Everyone should remember vital things to remember; this would not mean they are hiding something from you. On the opposing, those people trying to get rid of people's reason behind this is they might be trying to escape from you. When peoples close their eyes, you should go.

When someone Covering the mouth with a hand

This is one of the prominent notice that we all had a childhood in life. So, can you recall? You at all times cover your mouth if you did didn't want to tell somebody how you feel or anything else. It happens when we grow up in life too. A few fingers and a palm, even a fist near the mouth, would help us not to release the words we never wanted to want to say.

Sometimes this is a sign that is masked by fake coughing.

Citing the arms of their glasses

We can see when a person is sharp the arms of their glasses. We should try to support them and cheer them up always. Those people are usually concerned about some small matters unconsciously. Those people are trying to feel safe about themselves like they were, especially when their mothers were breastfeeding them.

Like a pencil and pen, a cigarette, and even when someone chewing gum in their mouth can specify the same thing.

Presentation of the face

This sign is used usually by the people to attract the opposite sex. Normally when we put our chins on our hand's people present our faces as when we're trying to say this is me. People can enjoy as much as their hearts want.

People should learn this sign to clasp the moment and give praise at the right time.

When someone Rubbing the chin

Rubbing the chin symbolizes the deep thoughts of a person. This happens when people are trying to decide something. This is possible when they might be looking down up and anywhere. They barely even know what and why they are looking at since they are deep in thought.

When they Crossed arms

This is one of the signs used commonly by the people. Many people feel very comfortable in this location. It will help them shut themselves off from those people. We sometimes use this gesture when we are annoyed by something from someone. When Crossed arms are a strong sign that a person does not touch good about something.

When we are fixing the appearance

When females want to get praised by their opposite sex, she tries to look herself in the best and imaginable way the way they are doing. She will unbend her back to highpoint her figure, and she will also cross her legs. Hands together and falling are a signal of care and enormous care in a person.

When leaning forward

This symbolizes someone's likeness toward the other person. When we want to make eye contact with the person whom we like, we usually lean forward. In this situation, the legs can be stationary, but the body will move forward automatically.

When you are leaning back

When someone leans on the spinal of their chair, it shows that the other person is exhausted from the chat. Perhaps they feel pain in the existence of the other person.

When someone swinging from heels to toes

This is not only done by kids. This shows that an individual is feeling nervous about something.

Rubbing hands

It is supposed that the hands always broadcast what is going on in our heads. When someone is rubbing their hands composed usually, it would mean that a person has an optimistic feeling about somewhat. They would be very confident. We can do this when someone is thinking about some profits impending in the future.

When Glove handshake

When you are depressed, and you are talking with a person who takes your wrist with their free hand, it is mean that you can trust them.

When you Handshake with a palm facing the ceiling.

A palm on top of individual hand indications that a person is feeling very concerned. Then this is true only when one fixes it quickly.

However, when a person has apprehended the handshake for some time formerly and only then does the other soul put their hand on top; this may be a mark that they want to express to you who is in custody here.

When you Handshake with a palm facing the floor

When you are holding somebody's hand from underneath, you want to tell them that because you are prepared to help.

Handshake with a touch

When People from time to time trace others with their free hands. They can drop the prepare, the prod, and the back of the other person. Such type of attack of isolated space means that a person lacks an announcement. The earlier the Touch to the chest, the more the person wants the business.

When you Fix the tie

The meaning of this sign is contingent on the condition. When a gentleman does this near a good-looking lady. It will probably mean that he adores her. Though this sign may also designate that an individual does not sense content. Perhaps he fibbed and just wants to leave anywhere he is right now.

Collecting hairs that aren't there

This is a supposed movement gesture. Persons frequently use it to express that they are upset about somewhat, but they don't want to express it. In other words, they don't share their view obviously, but they are certainly affected by somewhat.

Putting feet on a desk

Such type a gesture may express a lot of things: bad manners, trying to show who the boss is, disrespect, or even that people care about their health. A psychologist believes that if you feel comfortable with such a position, then you should not rest like this anywhere but home.

When someone Mounting a chair like a horse

Well, the chair is not a horse, and even though its back remotely looks like a shield, it serves a different purpose. Many people are annoyed by others sitting like this because they feel the violence automatically. This condition is popular among leading people. If you don't want to appear weak, remain standing while they are riding their horse.

When someone Playing with a shoe

Crossed legs are one of the gorgeous lady positions. When a beautiful woman is playing with her scandal. She is trying her best to catch your consideration of her legs. This sign designates that a woman is peaceful and feeling very comfortable. This is one sort of green light for a gentleman.

While making Eye contact

The eyes are the clear mirror of the soul and a great way to communicate. A person can understand and read all the emotional states and sentiments of a person visible in their eyes.

People who love each other look at one another in the eye, hopeful to see the acolytes become better. In detail, it's very informal to sign because pupils can be up to 4 times superior associated with their usual state. When a person is annoyed, their eyes look like droplets since the acolytes get very small. You can easily understand what's going on.

Be objective and flexible

Beforehand someone effort to read people. They must have just the first repetition, having an open mind. The person sentiments and past pieces of knowledge impact your imitations and sentiments. When you critic people very easily. It will reason you to misjudge people. Be objective in imminent every communication and situation. Reason alone won't tell you the entire story about anybody. You must submit other energetic forms of evidence so that you can study to read the significant non-verbal inutile cues that people give off.

Pay attention to the appearance

When reading others, people should try to notice people's entrance. What are they trying? Are they dressed for their success, which specifies they are determined? Or they are wearing a t-shirt and jeans, which means they are feeling coziness. Do they have a pendant around the neck, such as a cross and Buddha, which designates their divine standards? Whatsoever they wear. People can always sense something from it. These are belongings people select to display with their entrances, such as a t-shirt with slogans and tattoos, including rings.

Pay attention to people's attitude

A person's attitude would say a lot about their personality. When they are gripping their head high, it will indicate they are self-confident. If they walk indecisively or shrink, it may be a sign of low confidence. We should notice and observe their physical movements. You can have a better idea about them more than say more than words, and people express their emotional state through actions.

When someone tries to interpret facial expressions

If you are a very master of the poker face, your sentiments will be imprinted on your face. According to the, there are numerous behaviors to understand facial languages. They are When someone sees cavernous frown lines starting, it will be suggesting the person is concerned, and might be possible he/she is overthinking. On the incompatible, an individual who is truthfully smiling will show crow's feet the beamlines of happiness. An additional thing to watch out for is pursed lips, which can signal anger, contempt, or bitterness. Moreover, a compressed jaw and teeth crushing are signs of tension. They are reward smile, and Lips dragged straight up, hollows at the flanks of mouth and eyebrows lift. This connects an optimistic response. Affiliative beam It will Contain persistent lips composed though also creation little hollows at the side of the mouth. Sign of friendship and taste.

Supremacy smile: Upper lip is raised, and cheeks get pushed upwards, the nose gets crumpled, hollow amid nose and mouth excavates, and elevated upper lids.

The person should not run away from small talk. Maybe you touch nervousness with small talk. Though, it will give you the chance to acquaint by hand with the other person. Small talk will help you detect how an individual acts in normal circumstances. You can then use it as a standard to precisely spot any conduct that is out of the normal.

WOMEN BEHAVIOR AND DARK PSYCHOLOGY

Dark psychology is usually linked with the exploited behavior of people. These types of behavior are perceived very negatively. They often complete successfully for power and resources, and it highlights usually for men, but the samples of women with diversities can also not be neglected. The women's associative behavior that is very antisocial and the trade that hypnotizes and underestimates women's ability to receive and be evil is often taken in very fewer women exploit others, yet all of our population don't expect a woman to be threatening. They are often taken very positively, softly, and non-threatening, and even if the women cause harm it is minimized, and women are very less responsible for the reactions, and also they are very less held responsible for the actions and because of the reason women even have done because the behavior is so unexpected.

This is the reason women think whatever they do, they can always gain sympathy in front of society, which is not necessary but somehow true.

Not everybody knows this dark psychology horror. It would benefit the women, or if they are aware of the darker side of themselves, they are afraid of the headed monster, and they often don't like to talk about this Complex topic where it is often said that women are the worst Enemies of other women and themselves.

It is very weird to listen to this and talk about it where it is it is one of the highest growth of society nowadays. Women's empowerment is stronger than any other Era. People are more liberal and more vocal about women's empowerment. They talk about it more openly, and the topic of feminism is so wide and addressed and portrayed in such a beautiful way that everybody comes ahead to give their part and add; however, there is something inside every woman that reacts against their kind that goes against their own will.

How it may not look wrong; however, the journey is not so easy, which is a lot of people say that it's a woman who breaks down another woman. Downgrading other Downgradingby by life can be hard sometimes anywhere pulling Each Other back. We don't think of it often, and it is a very innocent reality that we are not aware of. it remains in their selves. Town selves' personality is not only negative, but it is demeaning and is taken as negative because that is how we perceive, and we know it is a fact that we experience space at every stage of life, but we don't discuss that. We should not discuss because that is what women empowerment is all about human behavior should be controlled, and the darkest psychology of the women should also be understood and taken in charge as it is taken in charge of the men. With men, women can also be harmful when it comes to this as compared to men.

- **Gossiping:** There is no boundary set by dark psychology for the people. That's the same with the woman. the backbiting and the gossiping nature are the basic nature of the women it has no boundaries which are defined fun in doing so ever they don't care if anybody sentiments are being hurt while they are being hurt and women tend to talk so disgustingly about other women's that they find it entertaining however it is very shameful because they don't understand how much attention-seeking it is. It is often taken as a trait of women; however, they don't understand how attention-seeking it is and how embarrassing it gets, which is no matter if people are enjoying this attention, but it still looks really bad. Gossiping might look fine but can ruin another person's reputation because nobody is born a perfectionist, and nobody is born Evil. They are good on the inside; however, if a person is spreading rumors about someone, it can ruin the reputation and affect them similarly, it can of the people themselves.

It is right to be fully solved. They are being offended because which is if a person is gossiping, for example, if they are gossiping and if they are confronted about their bad habit, they lose control. It does not mean that they stop doing it because it is not bound they won't do it that openly but they would still do it is because they feel there is nothing wrong in it and once they are pinpointed for it they would start to pull away from people instead of abandoning this habit of themselves. They are not that trustworthy to give out secrets to them, and they can also forget someone. When women are gossiping they don't know when to stop and what to say, and it can hurt someone genuinely, and it gives out negative energy from them, and that is one of the biggest things that women associated with the dark psychology give out so many negative Vibes from them that is not our society is used to of looking at the home, and when they have them too, they always think that they would be that sweet child of people when they are not.

• **BAD WORDING:** Usually, females criticize others without giving it a thought, and that doesn't take charge of everything. A woman is working to make another woman let down, and they don't feel sorry for it. Older women are bringing down the younger ones; younger ones do it to the old ones. It is an unhealthy practice overall. The funny thing is that whatever they say is so easily digestible to the people that they don't even ask them to shut up then and there. The most common practice of this is in every household between a mother in law and daughter in law relation and even the value educated people tend to do it and the thing that is the part of human nature, but they don't understand that can lead to something very aggressive, and still, they don't stop or refrain themselves from doing so.

• **GLARING:** Women are born with the most beautiful eyes, and so are men. The woman is praised for the eyes throughout their life, but it is one of the most typical characteristics of women. They glare others to their soul and give out dirty looks to everybody around them, and it is an incoming threat in general. We often talk about bringing changes in women's empowerment forever. They can do anything that brings joy to them, and they would judge another woman by clearing at the measure; it would make them feel any better.

But they do it so the other person can feel very uncomfortable and they find betterment in doing so and they would laugh out loud, later on thinking about it. This is a very belittle characteristic of every woman; however, they don't want to help the darker side of the personality, so as a result, they don't stop doing it.

- **INSECURE AND JEALOUS:** women are extremely unconfident as compared to men. The same thing arises when they are in fear of losing anyone that they are attached to or something that they want badly. They are very fragile, and in that situation, they suffer more emotional jealousy than any other, and it is found in any age of the women regardless of how old they are, and they can do anything to for it. They don't want to lose someone they love no matter what happens with that is how women react to certain situations, and insecurity and jealousy are quite common in them; however, insecurity turns into an extreme obsession if it is not taken care of.

- **COMPARISON AND COMPETITION:** It happens sometimes, that people are very competitive. These are the words in the personality that bring out the best outcome in people, especially women. It gets negative when what they do is demoralize and destabilize and push Each Other down when there is a cold war among them.

It just comes with a very competitive nature towards each other and then compares them with other women irrespective of any relationship and friendship. This happens quite often, which is why we are living in a place where there is so much competition going on everything is going so digital the competition becomes natural; however, there are two types of competition.

Among competitions, there is one healthy competition and one unhealthy competition sometimes, and women are competing against Each Other. they don't look at the outcomes and what it is going to bring that is why it brings out an unhealthy competition between them that brings out the worst in them. it is always necessary to hold the Horses of the demons that are hidden and powerful working in the dark side. They are always competing, and they need to know that everything is temporary, And harming anybody while working to get something is not something great to do.

- **BELITTLING:** the darker side of every human being gives them the feeling that they are superior to others, and they have nothing to do in their life when that happens to them is that they start thinking that the world revolves around them. They try to belittle others because it is very easy to do so instead of showing gratitude to them and they do anything to make others wrong, and when they are criticized or when they are shown the reality they won't do anything to make it better instead they always put other people down and want to preserve the superiority of them over others, and they always want to have the high status in front of everybody which is why what they think is necessary to do so to look better and everybody whereas they are just making a fool of themselves and this is quite toxic. Women cannot usually understand this behavior. People must admit and examine themselves which is the above dark psychology because it can disturb women's life and people around them because not every woman is like this.

But there are certainly some women whose darker side is more powerful as compared to the other side of their life every human being has a dark and light inside it happens women approach towards is how they see towards different things. Similarly, when feminism has become the talk of the town, women should understand that there is a light side of feminism and the dark side of feminism, and there is so much more related to the community, especially when their traditional ideas on the concept of femininity. It targets woman to a particular way of living in a particular way of actin however some women do not agree to The feminism idea and its criteria, and they never oppose their beliefs which are that living like a nice girl is not enough and it may be a pleasant experience to see what it takes to take the whole of the darker side, but they need to understand that feminine energy is such a beautiful gift for women to experience by the substrates woman to be only the underside of themselves and they are unaware of how the direct energy works but they just keep on falling into a pit hole.

Dark psychology not only has negative consequences, but, surely, it is a little eviler and some situations, and it takes a lot of pain to warn people about the negative side regardless of their sex. However, when women are usually warned about the darker side, that is more defensive about themselves, and when boys and men are warned about the female nature and the darker side, it is known as misogynistic. Which is highly debatable and an ignited topic at this time.

The darker side of female nature is not only labeled as dangerous but a lot of people even though it is very powerful and evil, but it is not as quiet at it because they think that women are generally not meant to be Evil, but the darker side as actually very destructive for themselves and it is disrespectful in a lot of ways and can cause damage that women can do in a lot of ways it can cause a lot of emotional and physical damage, however, the emotional damage is not taken as real damage.

No one can ignore this fact that women love attention. The word victim is often associated with the females, and the negative side is always said is a man who is programmed to be conquered and be violent and be more Evil as compared to the women however women also come out as violent acts, and they are great manipulators, and they also have a darker psychology side of themselves, but they generally take advantage of the stereotype that presumes that they are very innocent.

Generally, dark psychology consists of discussions about women's behavior. We can see the evil side is a little more controlling as compared to the positive side. However, there might be some positive aspects of the dark psychology that is concerned c towards women where it is not as discussed as openly because we don't have much awareness about that in the dark psychology brings out more negative aspects of certain things.

Similarly goes with the woman characteristics for everybody can overcome the dark psychology side by the right therapies by examining themselves and by knowing what is right for them because there is nothing wrong in compromise into things.

MEN BEHAVIOR AND DARK PSYCHOLOGY

This is a big shock for the readers that, Dark Psychology is real, and the majority of us are victim to it on a day to day basis without even realizing it.

Dark Psychology can be defined as the knowledge of manipulation and control over one's mind, to convince them to do whatever it is that you want them to do. The reason the word "Psychology" is associated with this concept is that people use tactics of coercion and motivation of the mind to get whatever they want. Most of us might not want to hear it, but covert manipulation is often used by people you trust and people you love. For the women reading this, it is important to be able to relate the way males behave around you, to understand whether or not they are using Dark Psychology's tactics of manipulation, coercion, and persuasion on you. To get what they want, men very often manipulate women in multiple different ways.

1. **Compliments:** They could flood you with love and affection to ensure you comply with their request out of love back. This means they will butter you up till you agree to whatever it is that they want you to do. They will make you feel like you might as well follow through with their request because they love you, and you love them back, even if you do not want to do whatever it is that they require. This could be something small as going to his new friend's house that you do not feel comfortable around, or even something more serious. People do not usually realize that 'giving out excessive love' is a manipulation tactic. It does not necessarily always have to be for something negative and dangerous, but it is important to recognize all forms of influence to make sure we are not being made fools of. This tactic is known as *Love Flooding* by some professionals;

2. **Giving of Gifts:** The male counterpart will start flooding you with gifts, for you to show some

reciprocation. This is because when someone gives you a gift, it is human nature to feel obligated to do something back for the, not only as a form of a thank you, but also to compensate for them going out of their way. This is exactly why some people use this strategy to get their way;

3. **Love Denial:** As the name itself describes it, it is the opposite of Love Flooding. The male counterparts in your life will withhold their affection from you, and stop giving you the loving attention, till you feel the need to do whatever it is that they want just so that you can get some love and affection back out of them;

4. **Complete Withdrawal:** This is one of the most obvious forms of manipulation. Love Flooding and Love Denial as manipulative tactics can still be sometimes not recognizable; however, the majority of people understand that when someone is avoiding you or is giving you the

silent treatment, they are manipulating you by guilt-tripping you and making you feel bad and induce guilt. Men that you love do the same to get what they want out of you. Dark Psychology recognizes this as one of the major strategies of manipulation;

5. **Lying:** This is the not so obvious form of manipulation as it is not that easy to recognize when you are or are not being lied to, until and unless you are aware of all the pre-existing facts of the matter. The males will straight up lie to trick you into doing something for them, and because you will not know the reality of the situation, you will be persuaded into doing it. There are other forms of speech that all also included in this form of manipulation. Besides lying, they can exaggerate a story out of context, or maybe even not lie completely but tell you a partial truth. That means they will choose to ignore or not mention important parts of the story or situation while narrating it. These will be those

parts that would make you not want to do something for them, and ignoring those parts will mean that they unjustifiably coerced you. It is not much you can do to prevent this sort of manipulation unless, of course, you go out of your way to make sure your male counterpart is being honest with you. However, usually due to the existence of love and trust, women do not do so;

6. **Semantic Manipulation:** Though this is not exactly lying, it is somewhat a passive form of it. What this strategy means is that the male will talk to you in words that have a double meaning. That means, they will use words that are assumed to have a mutual definition, and so at the end of the conversation, you will be thinking something else and agreeing to it, while the male will have meant something different. However, later on, you will not be able to back out of your words because you would have given your commitment, and out of guilt of hurting the other person, you

will have been manipulated into doing whatever it is that the man would have wanted you to do;

7. **Reverse Psychology:** It is human nature to want to do something you are told not to do. We see it in parent-child relationships as well. Similarly, to get what they want out of you, men will manipulate you by making you feel like you cannot do something. This will directly affect your ego and damage your self-esteem, and to restore it, you will want to prove them wrong. This will make you fall into their manipulative trap, and you will end up doing exactly what they wanted in the first place, even though they made you feel like it is something you are incapable of doing. For example, you meet a guy, and the guy shows interest in you, but you do not have any interest back. For you to be into them, they will say something in such a way that you will want to prove them wrong. This is a tactic to get you to spend more time with them, giving them more leverage into finding ways to ensure you hold

your interest. This is also the tactic used when a man plays "Hard-to-Get." They will make you take an interest in them by acting as though they are unachievable. This is the most communal policy used by men to make you take notice of them and desire;

8. **Restriction of Choices:** This is the last of the tactics/strategies/behaviors used and enacted by men to persuade and convince you to do whatever it is that they want you to do. It can be used in two ways, either to make you choose a choice they want you to make, or to make you avoid a choice that they do not want you to take. For the first way, what they will do is they will ask you to do something, and if you do not wish to do it, they will give you more options, however, they will be worse for you than the one you rejected in the first place. Although, in reality, you can simply ignore all choices and not do any of them; the male counterparts will make you feel like you HAVE to make a choice. So,

you will, in the end, go for the initial option given that they wanted you to do as it will seem to be the least bad one. Now for the latter way, what they will do is that they will give you certain choices in such a way that you will be distracted from the initial decision/thing that you wanted to do. This strategy of manipulation can be separated into a class of its own known as 'Distractive Measures,' however, it is still a subcategory of 'Choice Restriction';

9. **Mind Games:** As Google defines it, mind games are 'psychologically manipulative behavior intended to gain the advantage over one another.' It is used when there is a struggle between two people for one-upmanship, which is when one wants to feel more superior to the other. People carry forward mind games to manipulate the one they want to make inferior, so they either say stuff they do not mean, or even go to extremes such as embarrassing their counterpart socially. For example, sometimes husbands will taunt and

demean their wives in public gatherings only so that she loses her self-esteem and becomes someone who is more easily coerced back home.

Besides using manipulative tactics to coerce women in their life, men behave in ways and use different tactics of psychology elsewhere as well. The most prominent of these is in politics. It is no lie that the majority of the politicians of the world are male. Extensive research was done in the male-to-female ratio of politicians and state leaders, and as of December 2018, it was found that the participation of females in national-level parliaments at a global level was only 24.1%. And that includes the statistics of all those in Developed Nations. Developing Nations have an almost negligible amount of women participation in politics. The male politicians in such nations use dark psychological tactics of manipulation on the people they are supposed to lead. They use persuasion tactics to convince the nation that they are the ones they should vote for by heightening the people's emotional state.

Fascists specifically use these tactics by irrationally inflating the concept of patriotism. This is seen throughout history and even in current world affairs as well, for example, Adolf Hitler during Nazi times, and Narendra Modi in India, and Kim Jong-un in North Korea now. Not only this but to maintain the status quo, these men also convince the nation into believing that female politicians are not fit for this kind of job, as they are 'overly emotional, rash and incapable.'

TRICKS TO ANALYZE OTHERS AND CHANGE WHAT OTHERS BELIEVE

Create a baseline

People have their modes of conduct respectively. All modes are dissimilar and different in their way. This is so because everyone has its way of communication. People have different gestures while talking. For example, some people fold their arms while talking or some look at the floor. There are other gestures as well including stroking the neckline or jiggling the feet. These are very common gestures that we can observe in most of the people. People use these gestures for different reasons. Sometimes there is no reason at all and it is just their habit of communicating like this. When the person makes a mental starting point of others' normal conduct will help you.

Look for deviations

You need to be very attentive towards the contradictions between the starting line that you have created and the other person's words.

You might have observed that a person starts clearing his throat recurrently in anxiety. As he offerings some moderately small changes to your profitable preparation, he starts to do this. You will have to decide investigation further, asking insufficient additional queries than you would usually have.

We should Notice clusters of signs

The words give meanings and fulfill the purpose of communication if they are collective. We cannot comprehend meaning from an alone word. The same is the case with signs. We need to observe every sign so that you can comprehend meaning after collecting all signs. We have to combine and contrast all the signs and thus figure out the desired meaning or purpose. The person should have to notice that someone very deeply provisional slightly diverse than usual. It is important to see whether a person repeats the behavior in different groups or not. You must have to Continue to observe the person when networks with others in the area. How is that person changing his expression?

How he/she is behaving with others and way of talking with other people. How their body language is communicating.

Always look into the mirror

Other people's state of mind is reproduced by the mirror neurons of our intelligence. We are trained to read each other's language of the body. Other's smiles give a smile on our faces and other's scowl behavior triggers our frown muscles. When we tend to look at some celebrities we get attracted to them. In life, when your friend partner life member partner doesn't reply that behavior, this person could be transfer you a strong message. He or she is no more interested and don't like you they aren't happy with something you are doing, and you have done already.

Identify the strong voice

One of the most influential people is not continuously the one inactive at the head of the table. You should understand that Self-assured people have robust voices.

When you are about a conference room table and the most self-assured individual is likely to be the most influential on, by having extensive carriage and strong voice and a big smile. You should never complicate a loud voice with a strong one. You should classify the solid voice, and your probabilities for achievement will increase intensely.

Carefully observe how they walk

People lack self-assurance who do not have graceful actions and are unhappy in life. When you look such people you are likely to offer them help to gain self-assurance. It might be possible you will need to ask him/her more straight queries throughout a conference to jerk those countless thoughts to open.

Pinpoint action words

You should clearly understand what he is saying, which sort of words they are choosing while talking with you. Their action and word will be decided. This single word specifies that most probably your boss.

Action words proposal visions into the way an individual reasons.

Look for personality clues

Every person has a unique and decent personality. But there are straightforward explanations that will also help you tell additional individuals so you can read him or her precisely.

- Which type of behavior someone showing?
- Does he or she appear ambitious by relation and importance?
- How would the person handle danger and doubt?
- How are they feeding his or her ego?
- What sort of behavior the person will show earn he /she will show extremely stressed?
- What sort of behavior the person will show earn she is extremely happy?

Person Should Start with Generational Differences

You should clearly understand when somebody's group will give you a dream about how he or she will think about it. It's a lens finished in which they would view life.

They would not be home worth in head-on communication. The Boomers, on the other hand, like to talk to somebody in person. Some expert says considerate somebody's generation will help you so much know the best method to method them to grow an affiliation. When we are closing a deal with a utopian. We should know there is no need to fly out and agenda a roundtable she says. They always favor a performance via the Internet. Boomers we spend the money so we should go out.

You should Recognize Hot Buttons

An additional way to tell what someone is rational is to look for their pain points, which would include asking the right queries.

Some expert says it's vital to establish an individual promise to get to know what they consider to be important in life.

When you have big ears and a small mouth.

What activates emotion for them? Where they have their comfort zone? She will ask you. You must have to have large ears and a small mouth. Some propose that hopping pre-canned chats and incoming the relationship as a conversation. You should ask open-ended questions would allow the individual to share their strong point and tests in life. And also, they should share stories about what they have done for others in their life—twenty times out of 100. The people will agree that they are having the same subject, which would very help you better comprehend what they need.

You Should Contemplate Personalities

It will help to your notice and observe separate potentials to control who they are as an individual and what's significant to them. Some expert says she/he very logical, and she tells well when people systematically lay out their thoughts I have taught my team that they have to come to be prepared to back up their inventiveness with statistics and if you don't, you've lost me also.

Look for clues into someone's character by paying attention to features and redundancy. Someone who chooses to be principal, for example, might have an overly firm handclasp, says Miner. People who welcome humor will often insert irony into a discussion. Use these clues to determine their morals and approach.

Look for Nonverbal Communication

Nonverbal behavior is also very important, some expert viewing for body language clues. When someone leans in, they are engaged.

When they back up and look down, when they turn away, they are not connecting to what you are saying. It's important to growing a good ear that can attend for the understated sounds of how they are saying and what they are saying. There is a quality of voice that can also deliver symbols. But when somebody is replying to you in drone, they are most likely uninterested in your idea what you are saying and not engrossed. When they look at you when you say and move earlier. When they are discovery value in what you're saying.

You should Be A Good Listener

The person should always listen to what an important person is saying as well as what they're not saying. This would be very harder when the conversation is made over the phone. Nobody says an engaged and eager voice is understandable. It's also apparent when someone is frustrated.

The person should detect their tenor vicissitudes, and you will hear an exhalation. You should also comprehend what is energetic to grow a good ear that can listen for the understated sound. Whatever dangerous and what it will comprise sensitivity should never be connected by email. When somebody picks up the phone, Emails are terrible for transmission, meaning behind the arguments. They can be a real intrusion to being subtle.

Always Pay Attention to Appearance

Attention to appearance plays a vital role. You need to pay attention to what type of clothes someone is wearing. You need to check are they wearing some appealing and powerful dress or not? If someone is wearing a top with cleavage then it means that she has a seductive choice. A pendant such as a cross or Buddha indicates mystical values.

Notice Posture

When reading people's posture, you should always ask yourself. Are they holding their head high, self-assured? Or do they walk irresolutely or shrink, a symbol of little sureness? Do they boastfulness with a puffed-out chest, a symbol of a big personality?

Always watch for Physical Movements

When are you leaning and distance and Observe where people lean? Usually, we lean near those we like and absent from those we don't. When someone Crossed arms and legs, it will mean this posture proposes defensiveness and anger, and self-defense. Normally When people cross their legs, they incline to point the toes of the top leg to the person they are most at ease with. When you are hiding one's hands. When people were dwelling their hands in their circuits, pouches, and they put them behind their backs, it suggests that they are hiding somewhat.

Lip biting and cuticle normally picking when people taste or lick their lips or pick their cuticles, they are annoying to calm themselves below weight or in an uncooperative condition.

Always Interpret Facial Expression

Feelings can become imprinted on our expressions. The expert suggests worry or over-thinking. Crow's feet are the beamlines of joy. Wrinkled lips signal annoyance, scorn, and anger. Teeth grinding and clenched jaw are signs of tension.

The Second Technique: Listen to Your Intuition

The person can tune into someone outside their body language and arguments. Instinct is what your gut textures, not what your skull says to you. Its nonverbal info you observe via images and ah-has, somewhat than reason. When you want to understand somebody, what totals the most is who the person is, not their outer trappings. Intuition lets you see additional than the clear to disclose a better-off story.

People should always Honor their gut feelings

People should always listen to what your gut says, particularly throughout first conferences, an instinctual response that happens beforehand you have a chance to think. It communicates whether you're at comfort or not. Instinctive spirits happen rapidly, an original reply. They're your interior fact rhythm, communicating when you can have faith people. People should never underestimate their guts.

When you are feeling the goosebumps

Goosebumps are wonderful spontaneous stings that take that we reverberate with persons who change and stimulate us or are proverb somewhat that raids an agreement. Goosebumps also occur when your knowledge praise that you've known someone beforehand; however, you've never met.

People should always pay attention to flashes of insight

In chats, you may beg about people who come in a showy. You should stay alert from them. Then, you might miss it. We tend to go onto the next supposed so fast these dangerous insights are lost.

Watch for innate understanding

When occasionally, you can feel people's bodily indications and emotions in your body, which is a penetrating form of understanding. So, when are you reading persons, notice? How my back hurt when it didn't before? Am I unhappy and upset after a boring meeting? To control if this is empathy, get feedback.

Always Sense Emotional Energy

The Feelings are a spectacular look of our vigor. We list these with instinct. Some people texture good to be about. When they recover your nature and vigor. Others are demanding. You impulsively want to get absent. This understated vigor can be felt creeps and feet from the body.

However, it's imperceptible. In Chinese drug, it's called chi, an energy that's vital to health.

Sense People's Attendance

This is the general vigor we emit, not unavoidably corresponding with arguments or behavior. It's the open atmosphere nearby us like a volley cloud or the sun. As you read, people sign. Do they have a friendly attendance that entices others? When you get the jitters and make you back off?

Always Observe Watch People's Eyes

Our eyes convey influential vigor. Just as the intelligence has an electromagnetic signal spreading outside the body, educations elect that the eyes scheme this too. Take time to detect people's eyes. Are they kind? Sexy? Calm? or Angry? You should also observe: Is here somebody at home in their eyes, characteristic a volume for familiarity? And do they appear to be protected and beating?

Notice the Texture of a Handclasp how they Hug, and Touch

We should share expressive energy over bodily interaction, much like an electrical current.

The person should ask yourself, does a handclasp or hug feel sincere, contented, self-assured, and is it off-putting, so you want to remove it.

Always Listen for Tone of Voice and Laugh

The quality and capacity of the voice can depict the true level of emotions. The frequencies of sounds create feelings that you can observe and sense by reading people's tone of voice that affects you. Ask yourself, does their tone feel calming. Is it rough, irritable, and whiny?

Tricks to change what others believe

It is very important to start with yourself if you want to bring change in others. You need to make sure that the things that you want to alter are those that you do efficiently.

When you will be central by example, your movements will help as a basis of goal contagion for other people in your setting. Your actions will influence others and thus they likely to copy you positively. Many lecturers we know make a point of employing in their workplaces with their doors open. They would perhaps be more creative custody their doors closed. The topic of working noticeably, though, is to give academics a sense of what is obligatory for achievement in the academe.

To equilibrium teaching lessons, when you are doing research, writing papers and reviewing papers for journals also writing grants, and doing managerial service for the college, most of the faculty know put in long workdays. Ability talks to their scholars about the rank of putting in this time, but it is calmer for scholars to adopt the effort wanted to prosper by sighted their ability counselors at work. When you involve in the same performances, you imagine others, and then you're showing the highest form of genuineness.

Suggest goals

A goalmouth is an end state that delivers a focus for your motivational energy. Goals that are distant in time need less energy than goals that are near in time. The more active the goal is, the bigger will be the influence on behavior. Consequently, you are prejudiced against doing things that will pay off in the long run when there is some other action you could do now to attain a short-term goalmouth.

When you want to help someone alteration, your task is to help him or her express daily short-term goals that will finally lead to long-term achievement and then help them recall those goals. They should think like a commercial vending a product. Most of the trades would never endure when they Vended a product to a person only once. People's actions are driven by exact circumstances. If your demonstration people the conditions in which the product is used finished say, an ad or product placement in a movie, then they will be repeated to use the product in those circumstances when they meet them later.

The same is true of taking less alcohol or getting more exercise, the goal is significant, but its assistance to be continually reminded of that goal. This could mean leaving little notes on the face of the fridge and hanging up the gymnasium bag in the lobby of the house.

Always Give the right feedback

The response can affect the attitude people accept about conduct and incentive. People frequently give others response that unintentionally strengthens their minds. Which tags activities as the result of secure characters. When you see a friend on a portion of food at a gathering ingesting a slight plate of berry, you would say to him. Amazing, you have strange determination, I'm unable to do on the insincere, and this is an admiration.

However, important this declaration is the idea that determination is an object that cannot be altered. The weight watcher might be showing great willpower in that disorder, but when he gives in to lure in approximately other disorder, does that now mean that he has touched the bounds of his determination. It is better to give an optimistic response to someone that does not strengthen an entity's outlook. For that same weight watcher, you say, "I'm awe-struck that you have achieved to evade all of these alluring puddings. What is your underground, You are still providing that an optimistic message, but you are not arrogant that there is some fixed volume for willpower? In its place, you're inviting him to tell you about all the strategies which he has put together to help support his success at sticking to his diet under difficult conditions.

This caring for response indorses an incremental mindset, which admits that most aptitudes are services that can be cultivated.

The reassurance you give also wants to be custom-made to a person's stage of change. Some expert proved through their research shows that positive and negative feedback have different effects on people. The positive feedback help to make the people more committed to a goal. The bad response is primarily good for encouraging people to make more expansion. When people are first preliminary to change their conduct, the optimistic response is valued since it helps them feel a better sense of promise near the goalmouth they want to achieve. These initial stages of conduct alteration can be a delicate time, so it will be helpful to strengthen the pledge to change. Over time, though, persons change their own rational away from their general promise to the goalmouth to their sense of development. In this stage, they are absorbed by negative feedback, which reminds them of the coldness between where they are now and would like to be. Of course, this negative response does not make people feel good. Smooth in the later phases of behavior change, people still enjoy getting positive response more than they like getting negative feedback. But at the end stage of the change, the optimistic feedback is not nearly as inspiring as the negative feedback. Though it can be problematic to give a type of bad feedback, it is significant to be eager to make people painful when employed with them to alteration conduct. When you're serving people achieve their vocations, then you can use uneasiness to help them get absorbed to seek a raise.

Schoolings propose that when you emphasize persons on the influence, they have complete at work. They are happy with their present job. Then they do not energetically pursue an increase. When you emphasize people on what left-overs to be attained in their vocations, then they feel bad about their present job but are absorbed to move to rise. Continuously repeat by hand that bad charitable response to persons who are previously dedicated to conducting change can branch them to recuperate.

Always Support good habits

A person should praise the qualities of lists in a variety of circumstances in which the same job has to be done recurrently. The expert talks about how one important source of contagions in infirmaries comes when a staff associate in the concentrated care unit has to put in a leading line. Which is a long thin pipe that's introduced into a mood in the torso so medicines can be transported straight into the circulation? When these lines get ill, it can put ICU patients who are previously quite sickening in serious hazard. Some expert suggests when a person in ICU. The ICU operate covers the enduring with a curtain when the streak is being introduced and uses chlorhexidine soap. Then the occurrence of these contagions goes down melodramatically. Hospitals in Michigan got a medicinal gear builder to bundle the drapes and the cleanser in a single tool kit and then gave the staff in the ICUs a list to make sure that they approved out each step in the similar instruction every time. This mixture of vicissitudes to the setting and routine shaped a reliable mapping that was recurrent often.

It dropped the occurrence of dominant line contagions to near zero, which greatly better patient consequences.

When Someone Want To alteration the conduct of the people around you, They Should think about how they can create reliable mappings in the setting. Are there approaches to receiving people to reorganize their environment in ways that will support the creation of habits? How Can you affect people to do an act often enough that they will get a habit?

When someone takes advantage of laziness

When Persons lack to minimize composed the amount of time spent rationally about their behavior and the amount of effort compulsory to perform. When you want to brand the required presentations as informal as conceivable to do and the unwanted performances firm to perform.

The humblest way to make this occur is to have a switch over people's settings. In some cities have bans smoking in offices and, indeed, in any community space. The employees must walk an extended method just to have a roll-up and which in numerous conditions makes burning very hard to do. There are additional habits to operate environments to hearten wanted performance. In some cities have connected numerous dog cleanliness positions all over town. These positions contain a trash can with a lining and a distributor with malleable that can be rummage-sale to choose up dog left-over.

These positions brand it easier for dog proprietors to spotless up after their dogs, which scratches down on the number of persons who are failed to do so.

WHAT IS EMOTIONAL INTELLIGENCE?

Emotional intelligence is a mixture of intellect and emotions through the use of emotions as sources of information that allow us to make sense of the social environment and manage it. Emotion refers to a state of feeling that conveys information about connections. The ability to observe the emotions of one's own and of others, distinguish between them, and use those facts to direct one's thought and behavior. Emotional intelligence states as an individual's ability to look after his or her emotions and also have the ability to empower other's emotions. In other words, it can also affect other people's emotions. Practically speaking, this means being aware that emotions can drive our attitudes and have an influence on people, either positive or negative, and getting to know how to control those emotions – ours and others, respectively – notably when under pressure.

Models of Emotional Intelligence

Emotional intelligence is a collection of structured skills that facilitates efficiently and accurately processing of emotionally relevant information. It is also recognized that emotional intelligence overlaps with standard tests grouped by the features of the Big Five: openness to knowledge, empathy, extroversion, congeniality, and neuroticism.

Four section models of emotional intelligence define the capabilities of different emotional intelligence areas. In concrete terms,

1. **Visualizing emotions** - It is the non-verbal processing of emotion and its meaning. Darwin claimed that emotional expression as a form of communication originated in animal species. As we know, in human beings, facial expressions are universally recognizable. The fundamental question behind communications research is how human beings perceive and express emotions. The ability to interpret correctly

provides a critical reference point for a more intuitive understanding of emotions.

2. **Expending emotions**- We use the emotions to make thinking easier. The feelings enter and direct the mind system as well as positive thinking. Emotions give priority to thought in pursuit of something that catches our attention. For certain creativity styles to emerge, emotions are critical. For example, the ability to carry out creative thinking required both mood swings and optimistic moods.

3. **Knowing emotions** - Emotions convey a message: joy shows optimism towards others; anger demonstrates an assault or damage to others; each emotion expresses its pattern of potential messages and behavior related to those messages. A message of rage means how people feel and are being handled. The feelings for action are correlated with specific sets of reactions. To the species' survival, it is important

to understand emotional messages and the actions linked with them. Understanding emotions include the ability to reason, along with other aspects, the detailed definition of emotions.

4. **Dealing emotions**- Emotions to convey information can often be controlled and understood. If they are not painful, a Person remains open to experience emotions and attempts to block those that are traumatic. Within the emotional comfort zone, it becomes possible to control, manipulate, and encourage the emotions of one's own and of others towards their personal and social goals. The mechanisms and strategies used to control the emotional self vary from person to person and circumstance.

Signs of Emotional Intelligence

Emotional intelligence is a continuum of learning and developing skills and behaviors. Here are some classic signs of low emotional intelligence people and high emotional intelligence people.

Individuals with high Emotional Intelligence:
- Realize the interrelationships between their feelings and how they act
- Stay calm and relaxed in a stressful situation
- Taking on hard people with patience and diplomacy
- Have the ability to influence and motivate others to achieve the target

Individuals with low Emotional Intelligence:
- Sometimes feel confused
- Have difficulties being self-assured
- Get distracted easily
- Get overwhelmed by feelings

Characteristics of Emotional Intelligence

Emotional intelligence can be an important part of how we communicate with others. Coworkers, colleagues, friends, family members, and other associates may sometimes be dealing with poor emotional skills that make social situations complicated and full of tensions. In other situations, your emotional intelligence abilities might even need a little training. Emotional intelligence is a primary leadership skill. Here are five main elements of emotional intelligence;

1. **Self-awareness**

   The first phase of emotional intelligence is self-awareness. It teaches how to recognize and be mindful of your emotions, their influences, and their effect. Self- awareness recognizes our feelings and reactions and understands them. People are very self-conscious who have high emotional intelligence in them. They recognize their emotions, but they don't let their feelings run over them because of that. They don't let their emotions go out of their hands and they have strong beliefs.

If you're self-aware of what you're going through, you'd be better able to understand others and have an impact on people around you. It also indicates you're also mindful of your strengths and weaknesses. Hang on to that moment when you feel rage and remember what made you so angry. It helps to keep a log. You will be willing to look at themselves genuinely too. You will know your strengths and weaknesses, and you will be working on those areas to help you to do better. Most people consider that the most important element of emotional intelligence is this self- awareness of oneself.

2. Self-regulation

Self-regulation manages, regulates, and adjusts our feelings, mood, responses, and reactions. Self-regulation can keep feelings and desires under control. Individuals do not make impulsive decisions that regulate themselves regularly. They think about it before they act. Thoughtfulness, ease with the change, honesty, and the capability to say 'no' are features of self-regulation.

Often when you feel feelings, you have little control over them. Nonetheless, you may have some control over how long an emotion will last through the use of some strategies to relieve negative emotions like anger, depression, and anxiety.

3. Motivation

Motivation is making use of our emotions to inspire us to take appropriate action, commit, follow-up, and work towards achieving our objectives. Usually, people with a high level of emotional intelligence are inspired and motivated. They willingly postpone immediate outcomes for long-term success. They are highly productive, they are always ready for the challenges, and they are very effective in everything they do.

It takes clear goals and a positive attitude to motivate you for any accomplishment. Though you may be inclined to either a positive or a negative attitude, you can learn to think more positively with effort and practice. If you capture negative thoughts when they arise, you can more actively reframe them in a positive manner — which will help you achieve your goals.

4. Empathy

Empathy is discerning other people's feelings, consider their emotions, and use that knowledge to respond more effectively to others. Perhaps this is the second most significant component of emotional intelligence. Empathy is the ability to recognize and console others around you with your wishes and perspectives. People with empathy are good at understanding other people even those feelings are not noticeable.

The potential to recognize how humans feel is important to your life and career success. The more capable you are of discerning the emotions behind the signals of others, the more you can monitor the messages you are sending them.

As a result, empathic people tend to be great at handling relationships, listening to them, and contributing to others. They prevent stereotyping and making judgments too fast and living their lives in a very open and honest manner.

5. Social skills

Social skills are building relationships, connecting with others in social situations, leading, negotiating disputes, and working as a team. That way of talking is likable in which you use good social skills that indicate your intelligence. People are fantastic team players with strong and good social competencies. Instead of focusing first on their performance, they are helping others grow and shine. They can handle conflicts, they are great communicators, and they master partnership building and maintaining.

The last thing is social skills, and this is one of the key aspects of emotional intelligence. Social skills are all about sharing your point of view. You can build a relationship with others that makes the relationship more secure. Developing successful interpersonal skills is certainly preferable for life and career success. In the ever-connected world of today, everybody has complete access to technical knowledge. So "people skills" have become even more important now because, in a global economy, you have to have high Emotional intelligence to better understand, empathize, and compromise with others.

Tips to improve Emotional Intelligence

1. **Use the active listening competencies** - In conversations, people with emotional intelligence listen for the explanation, rather than just waiting for their turn to talk. Before responding, they ensure they understand what's being said. They even take care of the nonverbal aspects of a conversation. They pay attention to a conversation's nonverbal specifics, too. This avoids misperceptions, allows the listener to respond correctly, and demonstrates respect for the person to whom they talk.

2. **Practice self-confidence**- People are said to be self-conscious and intuitive who has great emotional intelligence. They are aware of their thoughts and they know how these thoughts can affect those people who are around them. They often take on the thoughts and body language of others and use that information to improve their communication and skills.

3. **Have empathy for others**- those individuals can empathize better who is wise and intelligent. Empathy is said to be a strong emotion rather weak emotion. Empathy allows them, on a basic human level, to respond to others. People get attracted to each other when they have mutual trust. This trust can come through empathy and condolence.

4. **Employ an assertive communication style**- Assertive communication is going a long way towards earning respect without being too aggressive or defensive. Emotionally intelligent individuals know how to communicate their thoughts and needs openly while respecting others.

5. **Have inspiration**- Self-motivated people are emotionally intelligent, and their behavior motivates others. They set goals, and they're responsive to challenges.

6. **Use leadership qualities**- Emotional intelligent people possess strong leadership qualities. They have high standards and set an example for the rest. We have great decision-making and problem-solving capabilities and take the initiative. This makes a higher and more efficient performance level in both life and at work.

7. **Respond rather than reacting to dispute**- Emotional outbursts and feelings of anger are normal during conflict situations. The person with emotional intelligence knows how to remain calm in stressful situations. We do not make impulsive decisions, which can cause much greater problems.

8. **Practice techniques to keep a good attitude**- Do not underestimate the power of your actions. When an individual allows it, a negative attitude easily infects others. Those who are emotionally smart have an understanding of the moods of those around them and keep their attitude

accordingly. You should know what to do to get a good day and a positive outlook. This might include having a great breakfast or lunch, engaging in daytime prayer or meditation, or holding relevant quotes at their desk or phone.

9. **Be open and be sociable-** Those who are emotionally intelligent come out as easy going. They are laughing and showing off a positive presence. They use appropriate social skills focused on their connection to whoever they are around. They have excellent interpersonal skills, and we know how to communicate clearly, through oral or nonverbal communication.

10. **Handle criticism well-** A significant part of improving your emotional intelligence can take criticism. Instead of becoming insulted or angry, people with high EQ take a couple of moments to consider where the criticism comes from, how it impacts others or their success, and how they can resolve any issues constructively.

WHO SHOULD ACQUIRE EMOTIONAL INTELLIGENCE?

Emotional intelligence defines ways in which people empathize with their friends and do a lot of discussions. It helps us to build strong communication with others, better self-understanding, and a way of living a happier and healthier life.

Emotional intelligence is not yet fully understood; what we know is that emotions play a very important role in the human performance of our personal and professional lives, even more, crucial than our actual brain intelligence assessment. Although tools and technology can help us learn and master knowledge, nothing can overtake our ability to learn, handle, and control our emotions and of those around us. Emotional intelligence is not only for those who communicate and interact with other people, but it is a strong pathway to a healthy lifestyle. Emotional intelligence is very significant in every phase of life.

1. **Emotional Comfort**- Emotional intelligence influences our approach and attitude to life. It can also help relieve anxiety and avoid mood swings and depression. A high level of emotional intelligence correlates directly with a positive attitude and a better outlook on life.

2. **Resolve Conflicts**- When we can perceive the emotions of people and empathize with their experiences, it is much easier when they attempt to resolve conflicts or possibly avoid them. We're all the better at negotiating because of the very essence of our ability to understand others ' needs and desires. When we can understand what it is, it's easier to give people what they want.

3. **Achievement**- Higher emotional intelligence encourages us to become better internal motivators, which can minimize procrastination, improve self-confidence, and boost our ability to concentrate on a goal. It also helps us to develop better support systems, to resolve challenges, and to persevere with a more robust outlook.

4. **Physical Fitness**- The willingness to take care of our bodies and, in particular, to control our tension, which has a tremendous impact on our overall health, is strongly tied to our emotional intelligence. We can only expect to manage stress and maintain good health by being mindful of our emotional state and our responses to stress in our lives.

5. **Management-** The ability to identify what motivates people, to respond positively, and to build stronger working-place relations with others inevitably makes anyone with higher emotional intelligence better leaders. An effective leader should understand what his people's needs are so that those needs can be addressed in a way that promotes higher performance and satisfaction in the workplace. An emotionally sensitive and insightful leader can also build stronger teams by making strategic use of their team members ' emotional complexity to benefit the team as a whole.

6. **Relationship-** We are better able to communicate our thoughts more constructively, by better understanding and controlling our emotions. We're all able to better understand and communicate with those we're in relationships with. Knowing the desires, emotions, and experiences of those we care about leads to stronger relationships that are more satisfying.

Role of Emotional Intelligence in the Workplace

Emotional intelligence helps various areas of life, but in the workplace, it is especially important. Possessing the trait could take you further in your career. The ability to accept constructive, blame-free feedback will help you grow as an employee and succeed in your profession.

Emotional intelligence is advantageous in the workplace because you are less likely to make mistakes or poor decisions that might affect performance. Alternatively, you will use logic and reasoning to focus before responding to the implications of a decision. Emotional intelligence is central to a productive workplace. These people are more able to manage tension, solve problems, and collaborate with others.

Emotional business intelligence, or the ability to understand your and others ' feelings, is important regardless of where the company is in the market. By perfecting your emotional intelligence skills, you can gain a competitive advantage over others (and probably improve your income and job satisfaction) by working successfully with hard people and solving complex issues.

Emotional intelligence and the related skills of people are critical, as people are an important part of any enterprise. Emotions are vital pieces of information that need to be weighed when making decisions – even if that means knowing when to block them out.

Managing emotions is at the heart of the ability of people to be flexible and open to change, cooperate, seek input, take risks, deal with conflict, and perform under pressure. If emotions are not controlled, it will harm partnerships and collaboration, stifle innovation, and disrupt the success of an organization.

While the ability to use emotions to improve motivation and concentration includes emotional intelligence, it also includes the ability to disconnect from very powerful short-term emotions when required to better focus on the tasks at hand. Because of the powerful role that emotions play when managing strategies and engaging with subordinates, managers need to be particularly aware of and focus critically on their negative emotions that could emerge in the workplace. Leaders can improve their emotional intelligence by taking a moment to learn about people and getting more self-conscious of their own emotions. If you practice becoming more mindful of your own emotions and responses towards others, you will become more empathic.

For leadership positions, emotional intelligence is also useful. On the job, leaders oversee and manage people, and that trait helps make them accessible, powerful, and decisive. Emotional leadership maturity also implies an ability to deal with stressful situations and address problems without shouting or blaming others.

As it becomes increasingly important to hire the right workers in this competitive world, there are now some effective ways to sort out people who are qualified but also emotionally intelligent. Businesses and organizations have become highly aware that emotionally intelligent people usually make the best workers. A person with Emotional Intelligence is optimistic, empathetic, a very good communicator and listener, positive, willing to hand over high and lows of their days well, and someone with very good people skills and a difference-maker. You are self-actualized and high on the needs ladder of Maslow.

Emotionally intelligent leaders know how to handle tension in a way that motivates, rather than dishearten, their team. Also, they know why their team players are reacting in a particular way. Quality is sometimes linked to emotion, and leaders with emotional intelligence can discern what makes their team happy. Fostering a healthy environment may increase productivity.

Emotional intelligence is the ability to reason about emotions & emotional facts, and thought-enhancing emotions are essential to understanding the emotions of our own and others so that we can enhance interpersonal relations. High emotional intelligence is related to better job efficiency, better teamwork, increased innovation, employee engagement, and acceptance of the change. Beyond the workplace, emotionally smart people also enjoy better interpersonal relations at home.

Emotional Intelligence is one of the pillars of a successful life. And self-awareness is one of the roots of emotional intelligence. Emotional intelligence tells the people around you about your feelings and the world. It helps you to figure out the causes of your feelings and their response.

It's a tough task to develop emotional intelligence, but it's a great way to improve how you relate to others. One way of building emotional intelligence is to control your thoughts. Look at how your feelings interact with your emotions all day long. Thoughts release chemicals in the brain that drive things the way we do. When we realize the relation, we will work to reduce the negative emotions we feel by failing to give power to the thoughts that produce negative emotions, and by concentrating on that the thoughts we have that are connected to positive emotion.

Trust and emotional intelligence both play important roles in our social lives simply because they allow you to survive. You can't have your demands met without confidence. You're afraid to go up and start a conversation with someone. You cannot understand the emotional environment in the room without emotional intelligence.

You can learn emotional intelligence; it's a lifetime operation. Learning something is never too late; it only requires constant study and practice. Regardless of how old you are, you can still take up emotional intelligence and make your life better and healthier. Emotional intelligence is the key to creating healthy minds, making the best out of life, and establishing a safer world for behavior. With the dysfunctional state of the world today, our best hope for an optimistic future is emotional intelligence.

HOW TO ACQUIRE EMOTIONAL INTELLIGENCE?

Although "normal" intelligence is necessary for success throughout life, emotional intelligence is vital to relating to other people and accomplishing your goals. Numerous individuals accept that it is at any rate as significant as common intelligence, and innumerable organizations currently utilize emotional intelligence testing to employ new staff.

Emotional intelligence tells about your activities and feelings and how they can impact other people around you. It additionally implies that you respect others, listen in to their needs and demands, and can relate to them on a wide range of levels. It is also helpful in living a happy and satisfying life.

Individuals with high emotional intelligence don't let their feelings drive their activities or choices. They learn when their emotions are going to fall and, above all, they realize how to manage those feelings, so they don't contrarily influence any other individual.

Emotional intelligence is a mix of character features. Daniel Goleman, the psychologist, and writer who originated the field of emotional intelligence, recognized, and he classified four key components that characterize emotional intelligence:

1. Self-awareness
2. Self-administration
3. Social awareness
4. Relationship management

Emotional intelligence is a thing that accompanies being human in any event. A few people are born into the world with a high level of Emotional intelligence, while others fight to comprehend why they feel how they do, and can't get a handle on when another person is having a distressing day.

Fortunately, Emotional intelligence is a collection of character qualities, and they're all characteristics that can be strengthened with training and control. That indicates we all can work to improve our EQ.

Self-Awareness

Self-awareness leads you to recognize your emotions and make you understand your feelings and how they influence your thoughts and behavior. You know your abilities and weaknesses and have self-assurance.

Self-Administration

You're ready to control reckless emotions and manners, deal with your feelings in sound ways, step up, finish on responsibilities, and adjust to developing conditions.

Social Awareness

It is the ability to recognize how others are feeling. You can comprehend the feelings, demands, and problems of others, get on emotional signs, feel great socially, and observe the energy elements in an organization or association.

Relationship Management

You understand how to create and keep up great connections, communicate comfortably, motivate and influence others, work well in a group, and handle conflict.

Method To Acquire And Strengthen Your Emotional Intelligence

1. Know yourself

There are numerous ways to help your Emotional Intelligence; however, creating unique self-awareness is likely the most basic.

Self-awareness indicates knowing yourself: what motivates you, what you accept, what your traits are, what your feelings are, and, in particular, the "why" behind every one of these variables. For instance, for what reason do you have specific goals? For what purpose do you accept what you accept? Why would you say you are feeling along these lines?

Understanding yourself is the establishment of emotional intelligence.

One way to create self-awareness is to invest time when the day's end considering what you did and why you did it. Writing in a diary can additionally assist you in investigating your thoughts and feelings, and empower you to spot designs in your thoughts and conduct.

While you're considering or writing, give close attention to the thoughts, individuals, or circumstances that made you experience stress, anger, or disappointment during the day. What set off these forceful feelings? How could you respond? For what reason did you react that way.

Realize that emotions, all by themselves, are not terrible, and listing them like this can restrain your self-improvement. Instead, recognize and approve how you felt for the day, and invest time investigating the reasons for these feelings.

Another approach to support your awareness is to look for analysis from companions, family, and partners who won't be hesitant to come clean with you. Ask them to portray how they see you genuinely. This can be frightening for a few. However, their criticism can feature some significantly vulnerable sides you have about yourself. Relate how you see yourself with how others see you can assist transformational change. It's additionally useful to take a personality test, for example, the Myers-Briggs Type Indicator. A thorough personality test like Myers-Briggs will help reveal specific components of your personality that you may make some hard times telling all alone. This data can be incredibly enlightening. A personality test can likewise uncover vulnerabilities that you probably won't know.

2. Concentrate And Observe Others

Individuals with a high Emotional Intelligence invest a more significant amount of their time focusing on others, and less time considering themselves. They listen, relate, act with empathy.

Turning your thought outwards likewise enables you to see how others are feeling. When you notice a companion or partner is having a terrible day, you can connect and offer a listening ear. Regularly, essentially giving others the benefit of your time and attention can have a considerable effect. To concentrate more on others, start by becoming more compassionate. This indicates imagining someone else's perspective so you can attempt to feel what they're experiencing. However, it's insufficient just to observe things from their point of view. You additionally need to jump further and recognize the "why" behind their experience. For what reason is this individual inclination along these lines? What occasions may have driven them to think that way?

Next, be curious about others. Individuals with high EQ are more inspired by others than they are in themselves. Attempt to speak with others, particularly individuals you don't know or who are a bit different. Be curious and polite, and make it an activity to attempt to see things from their perspective honestly.

You likewise need to challenge your assumptions and even generalizations about others. Be conscious about how those thoughts may be forming how you cooperate with others.

3. Encourage Your Listening Skills

Individuals with high Emotional Intelligence utilize listening skills. This indicates they give others their complete attention while they're talking. To strengthen your listening skills, give others the benefit of your attention. Put down your telephone, make an effort not to get occupied by your thoughts or emotions, and don't invest any time "planning out" what you're going to state. Simply listen.

As you're listening, keep open chances and attempt to comprehend where the other individual is originating. Try not to pass judgment or make a hasty judgment. What's more, don't interfere. Imposing on others proposes that what you need to say is more important than what they're saying. After some time, this can be harming to your relationships.

Give close attention to the speaker's body language, facial appearances, and vocal tone. This will give you significant suggestions concerning what the individual is truly feeling.

It's likewise crucial to ask queries so the other individual can explain anything you don't comprehend. In addition to the fact that this helps you handle the full importance of what they're attempting to say; however, questions let the other individual realize you're focusing. Active listening requires practice, yet you'll likely observe a quick positive reaction from others when they sense they have your complete attention.

4. Acknowledge Your Mistakes

Individuals with high emotional intelligence aren't reluctant to acknowledge when they've committed a mistake, and they're rapid to apologize when they have to.

Acknowledging a mistake isn't simple in case you're not used to doing it. To begin, see how you've managed errors before. What happened in these circumstances? Did you blame another person, hide it where no one will think to look, or take responsibility for what happened? What was your opinion about your conduct after the incident was over?

It's important to recognize to yourself and other people, that you're not unique or perfect. Taking responsibility for every one of your activities, including your errors, encourages your honesty, and builds trust. People appreciate other people who show they are weak and are focused on making things right.

Another angle to this is standing criticism as a chance to gain some new useful knowledge about yourself. Attempt to set your emotions aside and search for reality in what the other person is saying (regardless of whether they're not conveying this input in an ideal manner.) What would you be able to gain from this criticism?

5. Take a Deep Breath and Think

Meditating no matter what your identity is or what you do, there will be times when you're in a charged or tense circumstance, and your fundamental nature is to respond without thinking.

Rather than saying something that you'll regret later, stop. Take a couple of full breaths, and name the feeling you're feeling. Essentially saying, "I'm feeling angry," or, "I'm feeling anxious," is a straightforward yet fantastic approach to hit the "delay" button, acknowledge how you're feeling, and, in particular, give yourself an essential minute to consider how you need to react to the circumstance.

6. Stop Judging

"Judge softly, if you should. There is generally a side you have not heard, a story you know nothing about, and a fight attempted that you are not battling." - Traci Lea LaRussa.

Individuals with high emotional intelligence make an effort not to pass judgment. The judgment of others, for the most part, occurs in a microsecond when thoughts like, "Amazing, that was an awkward move!" pop up in your brain. Subliminally, these thoughts cause you to feel better than the other individual. Indeed more often than not, we don't have the idea of what is going on with others. Rather than judging or offering a negative remark, take a full breath, and seek sympathy. Keep in mind; you seldom know the entire story. Assume the best about somebody. It feels good and doesn't cost much else.

7. Analyze Your Friendships

You have loved ones who continually complain, play the victim, and criticize others for their current situation, try to constrain your meeting with these individuals, and instead invest time with individuals who show a high level of emotional intelligence. Progress from their abilities, and copy the habits that impact you.

When you encircle yourself with individuals who cause you to feel engaged and inspired, you have the vitality and energy to do the same for another person.

8. Specify Your Goals

Reminder on notebook People with a high emotional intelligence recognize what they need to accomplish most in life since they know themselves very well.

Start by writing all that you might want to achieve throughout life. This may transform into a considerable rundown, so pick a couple of dreams you generally feel energetic about and apply the SMART goal setting strategy. Set an objective for this fantasy is Specific, Measurable, Attainable, Realistic.

To remain convinced, make a dream board. Set forth plainly, a dream board is an arrangement of pictures and words that keep your goal in your day by day view.

For instance, if you will probably take care of your home loan, you could make a dream board with photos of your home, smiling individuals living debt-free, and words that reveal how you would feel about having your home.

Break bigger goals into significant advances and make a system to begin. It's imperative to understand the part others play in helping you arrive at every achievement. Recognize their help and guidance, and say thanks to them for all that they're doing.

9. Take an EQ Test

You may think that it's helpful to take an emotional intelligence examination, for example, the one offered through TalentSmart. An EQ examination can give you your very own superior comprehension qualities and shortcomings, so you can rapidly distinguish the zones you have to chip away. An EQ evaluation shouldn't replace daily reflection; consider it a kick-off to increase your emotional intelligence abilities.

10. Become Aware Of Your Emotional Triggers

Another methodology Reece proposes for figuring out how to deal with our feelings is to identify the triggers that set them off in any case. This includes attempting to disconnect, predict, and control the parts of our communications with others that set us off.

A typical model is a thing that Reece calls the offense trigger. It depicts many people's capacity to get insulted by others' body language, their manner of speaking, etc. during discussions. The inverse is thinking about what their expected message maybe – possibly they're merely attempting to help.

We've identified an extremely extraordinary exercise for recognizing your triggers. The supporting inspiration for distinguishing our triggers is to have the option to control our intense maladaptive reactions to them. If we realize that somebody's ability to talk honestly will, in general, set us off, for instance, we can adjust our practices as needs be the point at which we cooperate with them.

Being less protective and forceful if cooperation is unavoidable, for instance, can assist us with arriving at a productive decision when we engage.

Effects Of Emotional Intelligence

People with high emotional intelligence can support you with exploring the social complexities of the working atmosphere, inspire others, and beat expectations in your job. When choosing an employee significant job candidate, numerous organizations currently rate emotional intelligence as substantial as the specialized job and utilize EQ testing before giving an appointment. Your physical wellbeing is essential. In case you are not dealing with your feelings, you are most likely not dealing with your pressure, either. This can lead to many genuine medical issues. Uncontrolled tension raises blood pressure, suppresses immunity, expands the danger of respiratory collapses and strokes, speeds up the aging process, and accelerates the risk of heart attacks. The initial step to improving emotional intelligence is to figure out how to manage pressure.

Your mental wellness, unmanaged feelings, and stress can moreover affect your psychological wellness, making you vulnerable to fear and sorrow. On the off chance that you can't understand, get settled with, or deal with your feelings, you'll likewise battle to shape stable relationships. This thus can leave you feeling miserable and separated and additionally fuel any sensitive issues.

Emotional intelligence helps you to figure out what are your feelings and how they affect others. It also helps you to control your emotions. This permits you to transmit more successfully and reproduce more reliable connections, both grinding away and in your own life.

Emotional Intelligence Benefits

1. Emotional intelligence causes us to deal with our feelings by permitting us to reject, disregard, or control our useless emotions in occurrences where they're simply not instrumental.

For instance, there's little an influence in shouting at a transport driver because your drive has been eased back somewhere around terrible traffic.

2. Our Emotional Intelligence capabilities are what permit us to understand and see how others are feeling. They assume a significant job in characterizing what our identity is by molding our associations with others around us.

3. Our Emotional Intelligence abilities are accepted to be huge supporters of our general achievement throughout life, because of their effect on our capability to self-manage and inspire.

A BRIEF INTRODUCTION TO MIND CONTROL

There's a science thereto. A man name of Dr. Robert Cialdini wrote a book referred to as Influence: The psychological science of Persuasion. He made public completely different principles scientifically well-tried to influence folks, yet as suggestions for a way to try and do it.

Since then, it's become perhaps the foremost vital book within the field of promoting. If you haven't search it, you should, yet because of the sequel.

Use these seven methods showing wisdom:
Here's why: folks have already got an excessive amount of to rely on. Add another sock, and therefore the whole can explode. To avoid it, they "forget" concerning things that aren't important to them, or if they are doing without relying on you, they don't assume onerously.

It isn't as a result of being lazy or stupid. They're simply busy, and you're most likely not high the priority list.

Begin associate degree avalanche

Creating a victorious promoting campaign could be a heap like beginning associate degree avalanche. The first huge affirmative could be a pain within the butt to induce, however, if you savvy from the proper person, then obtaining all of the next yeses is straightforward.

For example:

Getting a well-liked blogger to tweet your post is tough, however, once they are doing, dozens or even many folks can retweet them.

Convincing a pacesetter in your niche to push your product is hard, however, once they are doing, everybody else can need to push it too.

Persuading a celeb client to convey you a testimonial is powerful, however, once you are doing, sales skyrocket, and obtaining more testimonials is straightforward.

Yes, pushing over a tiny low rock is simpler than pushing over a boulder. However, the boulder could be a heap a lot of doubtless to cause associate degree avalanche. thus whereas it's a lot of add the start to induce high folks to assist you, it's really less add the long-standing time, and therefore the results square measure way, way larger.

For instance:

If you wish to jot down a guest post for a well-liked diary, begin by pitching the concept in one or 2 paragraphs, then send them an overview, then write the complete draft of the post.

If you wish to do a JV promotion with a pacesetter in your field, begin by asking them to email your launch content to solely 100% of their list, and then five-hundredths of their list, then 100%, then an immediate mail campaign.

If you wish your customers to convey your case studies, begin by soliciting for a 1-3 sentence promotion, then raise a half-page testimonial, then doing a two-hour webinar getting into depth about their success.

It's not psychological trickery or something like that. It's a sort of good business. Nobody likes to risk everything direct, and by providing progressive levels of commitment, your probabilities of obtaining them to mention affirmative undergo the roof.

Continuously have a true point in time

The keyword is "real."

All United States have had salesmen who tell us, "Well, you'd higher revisit to Pine Tree State quick, as a result of I actually have 3 a lot of prospects returning this afternoon, and that I don't shrewdness long, it'll last."

There are not any purchasers, and there's no urgency. And it's not simply salesmen. Our academics screw, our bosses screw, our family will it, and stupidly concerning it, you've most likely done it too.

Not solely is it ineffective; however, it's entirely spare. Real urgency is straightforward to form. With a touch thought, you'll be able to build it into your promoting. Not solely can you get a great deal a lot of downloads, however alternative bloggers are a great deal a lot of doubtless to push it throughout the window?

Instead of asking customers for testimonials whenever they get around thereto, show them the timeline for the associate degree forthcoming launch, as well as a particular date to channel testimonials.

And if you let people dictate timelines, that's specifically what's going to happen.

Offer 10 times quite you're taking

You know you're imagined to offer before you get, right? However, what you may not apprehend is proportion to convey. A lot of marketers awkwardly assume it's a 1:1 quantitative relation. Before you raise a link, you are necessary to provide a link. Before you raise promotion, you are necessary to provide a promotion.

If you wish one hundred guests, send them 1000. If you wish $1000 in product sales, sell $10,000 of their product initial. If you wish one testimonial, do 10 completely different heroic acts of client service merit a testimonial This isn't concerning "You scratch my back,

I'll scratch yours." It's concerning generosity thus overwhelming they can't say no.

Yes, it's a great deal of labor; however, that's the value of influence. The first guy includes a traditional, run-of-the-mine sign expression, "Spare many dollars? God bless you. Please facilitate this. I will stop feeling like such an associate degree awful pater."

Which one would you be a lot of doubtless to help? The second, right? Forget giving him many USD. With an indication like that, you'd take him to the foodstuff and get him $200 value of groceries. I do know. That's the ability to stand for one thing larger than yourself. It makes folks care.

And it applies to everything:
Instead of writing one more how-to post, take a stand on a crucial issue, conflict with each passion, and unassailable logic. Instead of starting point one more me-too consulting business, move, operating generously to vary the lives of your customers. Instead of industrialism, one more gradual manual, sell a philosophy, glutted with heroic examples to inspire your customers.

Those square measure the kinds of things household need to speak regarding. They feel grateful only for having the investigation to assist you in unbending the word.

Do you want to grasp what separates an excellent changer from a mediocre one?

Shamelessness.

I'm not bearing on a vacancy of conscience, having a companionable, personable temperament, or any of the opposite ways in which we tend to historically cross-check marketers. For the foremost half, those convention square measure fable. No, by impudence, I mean this:

An unsinkable belief that what you're doing is nice for the rondure and, therefore, the disposition to try and do something to bring it into being.

When you believe your peace, you don't publish it and forget it. You put up for sale day when a day, the week when a week, the month when a month, the year when a year, operating affluently to unwrap the message to everybody UN agency has to hear it and ignore to rest till they are doing.

When you believe your product, you don't resist sales. You enjoy it. Not as a result of you're greedy or furious or self-important, however as a result of you recognize your product can facilitate them, then it's your duty to induce them to shop for. no matter what it takes.

When you believe in charity, you don't beg for donations. You demand them. You capture folks by the shoulders and presentation them within the eyes and tell them what you're doing is dynamical the globe, and it's time for them to accelerate and do their half. It does not concern cash. It's not concerning glory. It does not even concern a gift.

It's concerning falling soft on. It's concerning being mesmerized. It's concerning seeing a vision thus stunning you can't facilitate, however, fight to form it real.

Our mind is powerful; nonetheless, we can manage it victimization mind management techniques. It is attainable to only implant an exact thought in our mind, and feel the emotions connected thereupon thought and to coach your mind to retort during a manner that we tend to need.

Every individual aims at happiness and pursues his or her path towards this goal. As people, our ideas of what constitutes happiness disagree.

PERSUASION

When you consider persuasion, what is it that comes to mind? A few people may consider developing messages that ask watchers to purchase a specific item. In contrast, others may think about a political applicant attempting to persuasion voters to pick their names on the voting booth. Persuasion is a ground-breaking power in everyday life and impacts society and an entirety. Political issues, right choices, broad communications, news, and advertising are affected by the intensity of persuasion and impact us. During some circumstances, we like to accept that we are indifferent to persuasion. That we have an inherent capacity to see through the attempt to sell something, understand reality in a situation, and arrive at resolutions entirely. This may be valid in certain conditions, yet persuasion isn't only a pushy sales rep attempting to sell you a vehicle, or a TV ad luring you to purchase the best in the class item. Persuasion can be reserved, and how we react to such impacts can rely upon a variety of components.

When we consider persuasion, negative models are frequently the first to comes in mind, yet persuasion can likewise be utilized as a positive power. Public help campaigns that urge individuals to reuse or stop smoking are extraordinary examples of persuasion used to improve individuals' lives.

What Is Persuasion?

So what precisely is persuasion? In The Dynamics of Persuasion, Perloff characterizes persuasion can be described as "...a typical procedure in which communicators attempt to persuade others to change their mentalities or practices concerning an issue through the transmission of a message in an environment of free choice."

The critical components of this meaning of persuasion are that:

- Persuasion is representative, using words, pictures, sounds, and so forth
- It includes a purposeful effort to impact others.

- Self-persuasion is vital. Individuals are not forced; they are instead allowed to pick.

- Strategies for transmitting convincing messages can happen in a variety of ways, including speaking person-to-person and nonverbally using TV, radio, Internet, or up close and personal correspondence.

Dark Persuasion

Dark persuasion lacks any motive. It is different from positive persuasion. This is characterized as the opposite if positive belief as hurting people without cause. Sometimes dark persuader thinks that he is wise and he should attempt such an act. The motivations of their actions depend upon the personality type. If they are from type B, they can be destructive. Dark persuasion has lethal outcomes. The person will take control of the other individual and influence them to commit wrong. And if someone goes against them, they can turn into evil and can victimize the individual. In many cases, victims lose their lives.

Dark persuasion tactics

How do persuaders fulfill their wishes? That depends on the method of persuasion. The long con is one of them. In this type, the persuader takes time to gain the trust if the victim. They will be friends first. After knowing the fact that the victim trusts them, they start to attempt their evil persuasion in them. This leads to making choices probably wrong by which the only persuader is getting the benefit.

HOW TO RECOGNIZE MIND CONTROL TECHNIQUES?

Have the proper business ideas? Attempting to induce individuals to come back to your event or party, however, nobody is RSVP-ing? Or, does one surprise a way to forestall you from obtaining scammed by salespeople? This journal post summarizes material from Henry Martyn Robert Cialdini's "Influence: The scientific discipline of Persuasion" and general psychological phenomena.

1. Offer, and You Shall Receive

Thank you, Costco, for being impressive. However conjointly sneaky. Reciprocity may be real stuff, and it very works! Costco is ill-famed for his or her for his or her you get a free sample, you're feeling a way of obligation to come to the favor by shopping for a product.

Researchers within the famed "Coca-Cola experiment" showed that reciprocity would work while not the recipient acceptive the gift. Participants were told to judge art and buy a self-selected range of raffle tickets. Participants UN agency were provided a free Coca-Cola liquid bought doubly the quantity of the quantity if they reduce the offer of the beverage!

2. A door within the Face and Foot within the Door
A door within the Face. First, enkindle an enormous demand. Then, raise the request you had originally wished. This technique is especially effective as a result of it makes the opposite person feel unhealthy for rejecting your 1st request. this can be the technique that Calvin is exploitation within the Calvin and Thomas Hobbes comic on top of.

Foot within the Door. Variety of the alternative of "Door within the Face" technique, this technique involves soliciting for a little favor 1st, then increasing the favor. For instance, rise if your friend can allow you to borrow their automotive for every day.

Once they agree, raise if they wouldn't mind disposal it to you for a few additional days, too. This technique is effective as a result of individuals who don't like breaking commitments.

3. Low-balling

This is the ill-famed technique utilized by most automotive salespeople. You and also the employee agree on a deal for $495. on the other hand, as you land up the payment method, there are some additional fees and supplemental costs. Therefore the total will increase to $1,000. You falter for a second. The employee disbelievingly inquires, "But, ar you about to modification your mind on this deal we tend to had?" afraid regarding breaking your commitment, you are saying, "Of course not!" and pay money for the automotive. This maneuver is effective as a result of it causes you to want you're ending a deal that have already been created, albeit the employee is surreptitiously sterilization the arrangement.

4. Social Proof

"If others do it, it should be right." the ability of social proof creates long lines for no reason likewise as additional sinister situations, just like the watcher impact. In general, if one thing seems as if it's already well-liked, it'll still become additional cogent. Social proof is a very common force within the business world. Tip jars seldom get further cash if there's no cash within the jar already. A typical trick? Place a number of your cash within the tip jar before you interact with customers. Or consider the video below, at a music competition wherever one man gets an entire crowd to bop.

5. Likability

This one is maybe the foremost obvious: if individuals such as you, they'll do things for you. A number of the foremost common ways that to become additionally likable:

- **Being engaging**
- **Being just like your audience**
- **Giving compliments**

- **Frequent contact**

Note that within the on top of the image, it's not entirely clear that one is additionally likable. Whereas Zac Efron on the left is the additional engaging, Seth Rogen is extremely relatable and sure additional just like the viewer, as opposition the god-like body of Zac Efron.

6. Authority

In the famed Milgram experiment, participants (the "Teacher") administered electrical shocks to a different person (the "Student") UN agency was performing arts a word try to exercise. The electrical shocks were pretended, and also the student was in on the experiment, dissembling that the electrical shocks were inflicting him pain. Associate "Experimenter" vie the authority within the space with the Teacher. Whenever the Teacher would be unsure regarding administering further electrical shocks, the Experimenter, sporting a laboratory coat, would urge the Teacher to continue.

The results were shocking: the overwhelming majority of participants continuing to administer electrical shocks to levels of fatality, once prompted by the lab-coated Experimenter.

The Milgram experiment is proof of the ability of authority. In general, having the associate authority of any kind will very persuade individuals. Simply take a glance at the Lucky Strike ad below. Even though doctors say the cigarettes are less irritating, it doesn't mean they're any higher for your lungs.

7. Scarcity

Making things appear additional scarce makes them additional fascinating. Individuals believe that they need a singular chance to induce one thing and that they don't need to miss out.

This technique is extraordinarily common within the marketplace world whether you're exploiting these techniques for your profit, to push an organization, or to set up events, keep in mind to be respectful of individuals and to not brainwash or exploit. I, in person, study these ways largely as a method of protection, to avoid being cornered in one amongst these "mind control" methods. Consider "Influence" by Henry Martyn Robert Cialdini for an additional in-depth understanding of those techniques and the way they work.

WAYS TO LEARN PERSUASION THROUGH MANIPULATION OF SOME TECHNIQUES AND UNLOCKED MIND CONTROL?

Persuasion may be a technique that you just use on a commonplace, however persuasive area unit you? Area unit you obtain what you're seeking once trying to steer others? If not, it's time to begin functioning on your ability to steer. It's typically thought that persuasion, and therefore the techniques that makeup it, is barely used for selfish reasons; however, this can be not true. Being smart at persuasion is required to induce ahead at work, kind friendships, and even once interacting with strangers.

Persuasion maybe a talent and one that you just will develop with the correct tips and knowledge. This book is the beginning of taking the mandatory action to enhance your persuasion skills. It starts with the fundamentals of persuasion and permits you to assess, however effective you presently area unit. From there, you may get many unjust tips to boost your ability to steer others.

Study techniques and the way to use manipulation techniques to your advantage. The mental state is next. This can be a fascinating talent to own as a result of it's not a standard one. It's one thing which will aid you in obtaining a lot of what you would like from individuals and your life.

This can be a talent you would like to amass to assist with a lot of advanced persuasion skills. This can be followed by learning concerning deception and what you'll be able to do to enhance your skills and utilize this persuasion technique to your advantage.

Mind games and mind management area unit consecutive skills you may study. You may be shocked concerning, however, these area units are utilized in daily life. You possibly fall victim to them quite frequently in ways that you're not even awake to.

Brainwashing somebody or exploitation powerful persuasion isn't straightforward. It consists of closing the topic far from the globe mentally, socially, and physically. In alternative words, utterly uninflected the individual.

With less data, the topic won't have as several choices to decide on from. Their essential thinking also will be restricted. Usually, that somebody could be a reasonable leader. In observe, it suggests that satisfying someone's primary and secondary desires until there's a complete dependency.

Psychophysical enervation: Some varieties of physical enervation area units are related to psychological debilitation. Individuals use it to draw individuals in and grab their attention.

Cognitive techniques: These varieties of techniques drawn from the 2 we tend to already mentioned.Denigration of essential thinking: The culprit shows the individual the illogicality of following their thoughts. Thus, when they assume one thing, they find yourself inhibitory.

Use of deceit and lies: Distorting reality by activity data, lying, or deceiving. As a result, people lose their temperament and war the group's identity. this may build people to lose any characteristic characteristics. Omitting bound words or phrases is a way of avoiding explicit queries or analysis.

Changing the supply of authority: Once you level a person's principles of authority, you expose them to a totalitarian authority. Consequently, this authority gains all the ability. Everybody else has got to submit.

"There are a unit solely 2 suggests that by that men will cope with one another: guns or logic. Force or persuasion. People, who understand that they cannot win by suggesting that of logic, have forever resorted to guns."

A guy cornered in an exceeding hole by powerful persuasion. These states of consciousness conjointly build followers a lot of vulnerable. As a result, it's easier to manage them by limiting their choices and reducing their ability to judge them. Psychological features and emotional persuasion amendment the approach they assume and feel.

Social influence isn't essentially negative. Social influence is mostly looked as if it would be harmless once it respects the proper of the influenced to simply accept or reject it, and isn't unduly powerful. Counting on the context and motivations, social influence could represent dishonest administration.

Negative Brace: involves removing one from a negative state of affairs as an award, e.g., "You will not have to be compelled to do your prep if you permit Pine Tree State to try and do this to you."

The partial or intermittent positive brace will encourage the victim to persist – for instance, in most varieties of action, the bookmaker is probably going to win currently and once more, however still lose cash overall.

According to Simon

Simon known the subsequent artful techniques:

Lying (by commission): it's exhausting to inform if someone is lying at the time they are doing it, though typically the reality could also be apparent later once it's too late. a technique to constrict the possibilities of being a song is to know that some attitude sorts (particularly psychopaths) square measure specialists at the art of lying and cheating, doing it ofttimes, and sometimes in delicate ways that.

Selective basic cognitive process or selective attention: Manipulator refuses to listen to something which will divert from their agenda, spoken language things like "I don't need to listen to it."

Evasion: just like a diversion, however, giving extraneous, rambling, imprecise responses, most lined mammal words.

Guilt trip: A special, reasonably coercion maneuver. Shaming techniques are often terribly delicate like a fierce look or look, unpleasant tone of voice, rhetorical comments, and delicate satire. Manipulators will build one feel guilty for even daring to challenge them. It's good thanks to foster a way of inadequacy within the victim.

Vilifying the victim: quite the other, this maneuver could be a powerful means that of golf stroke the victim on the defensive whereas at the same time masking the aggressive intent of the manipulator.

Whereas the manipulator incorrectly accuses the victim as being an Associate in Nursing maltreater in response once the victim stands up for or defends themselves or their position.

Playing the victim role: A manipulator portrays themself as a victim of circumstance or somebody else's behavior to achieve pity, sympathy, or evoke compassion and thereby get one thing from another. Caring and conscientious individuals cannot stand to examine anyone suffering, and also the manipulator typically finds it straightforward to play on sympathy to induce cooperation.

Playing the servant role: Cloaking a self-seeking agenda within the pretense of a service to a lot of noble cause, spoken language they're acting in a very sure thanks to being "obedient" to or in "service" to a force or "just doing their job."

Seduction: Manipulator uses charm, praise, admiration, or overtly supporting others to induce them to lower their defenses and provides their trust and loyalty to the manipulator. They're going to additionally provide facilities with the intent to achieve trust Associate in Nursing access to an innocent victim they need to be captivated.

Projecting the blame: Manipulator incriminates in typically delicate, hard-to-detect ways that. Often, the manipulator can project their thinking onto the victim, creating the victim appear as if they need to do one thing wrong. Manipulators also will claim that the victim is that the one World Health Organization is guilty for basic intellectual process lies that they were conned into the basic cognitive process as if the victim forced the manipulator to be deceptive. All blame, apart from the half that's utilized by the manipulator to simply accept false guilt, is completed to create the victim feel guilty concerning creating healthy decisions, correct thinking, and smart behaviors.

It's often times used as a method of psychological and emotional manipulation and management.

Manipulators laze lying, solely to re-manipulate the initial, less conceivable story into a "more acceptable" truth that the victim can believe.

Outstanding lies as being the reality is another common methodology of management and manipulation. Manipulators like to incorrectly accuse the victim as "deserving to be treated that means." They typically claim that the victim is crazy and/or abusive, particularly once there's proof against the manipulator.

Manipulators could be placed on a glance of surprise or outrage. This maneuver makes the victim question their judgment and probably their mental health. Generally, manipulators can have used cohorts before to assist duplicate their stories.

The manipulator isn't truly angry, and they simply placed on Associate in the Nursing act. they simply need what they need and obtain "angry" once denied. The victim becomes a lot of centered on the anger rather than the manipulation maneuver.

These embrace phrases like "Many individuals such as you ..." or "Everyone will this anyways.

Susceptibility exploited by manipulators

According to Braiker's assist book, manipulators exploit the subsequent vulnerabilities (buttons) which will exist in victims: the "disease to please "addiction to earning the approval and acceptance of others Emetophobia (fear of negative emotion; i.e., a concern of expressing anger, frustration or disapproval) lack of positiveness and skill to mention no blurry sense of identity (with soft personal boundaries) low self-sufficient external locus of management According to Simon, manipulators accomplishment the subsequent vulnerabilities which will exist in victims

Over-conscientiousness the victim is simply too willing to convey manipulator the good thing about the doubt and see their aspect of things during which they blame the victim.

naïve – cannot believe there square measure dishonest individuals within the world or takes it without any consideration that if there square measure any, they're going to not be allowed to go after others.

Impressionable too seduced by charmers. for instance, they may vote for the ostensibly charming politician World Health Organization kisses babies.

Trusting: Those who square measure honest typically assume that everybody else is honest. they're a lot of doubtless to commit themselves to individuals they hardly grasp on faith credentials, etc., and fewer doubtless to question supposed specialists.

Carelessness not giving a sufficient quantity of thought or attention to hurt or errors.

lonely: Lonely individuals could settle for any provision of human contact. A psychopathological trespasser could provide a human-friendly relationship for a value.

Narcissistic: Narcissists square measure vulnerable to falling for the unmerited compliment.

Altruistic: The alternative of psychopathic: too honest, too fair, too sympathetic.

Frugal cannot say no to a cut-price, notwithstanding they grasp the explanation. It's therefore low in cost.

Greedy: The greedy Associate in Nursingd dishonest could fall prey to a psychoneurotic World Health Organization that will simply lure them into acting in an immoral means.

Masochistic lack dignity and then unconsciously let psychopaths benefit from them. They assume they merit it out of a way of guilt.

The old will become worn out and fewer capable of multi-tasking. Once hearing a sales talk, they're less doubtless to contemplate that it may be a con.

They're vulnerable to giving cash to somebody with a hard-luck story. See elder abuse.

Motivations of manipulators

Manipulators will have numerous doable motivations, as well as however not restricted to:

- They need to advance their functions and private gain at nearly any price to others.
- A strong got to attain feelings of power and superiority in relationships with others.
- A need and wish to feel up to the mark.
- A wish to achieve a sense of power over others to lift their perception of shallowness.
- Boredom, or growing uninterested in their surroundings, seeing it as a game quite pain others.

Covert agenda, criminal or otherwise, as well as monetary manipulation (often seen once the old or unsuspecting, unprotected flush square measure deliberately targeted for the only real purpose of getting a victim's monetary assets) not distinctive with underlying emotions, commitment-phobic disorder, and later rationalization (offender doesn't manipulate consciously, however rather tries to convert themselves of the illogicality of their own emotions).Lack of self-management over impulsive and anti-social behavior so pre-emptive or reactionary manipulation to take care of image.

Main article: A psychological state within the geographical point:

One approach to management normally identifies a really fine, nearly non-existent line between management and manipulation.

The geographical point psychoneurotic could typically apace shift between emotions – accustomed manipulate individuals or to cause high anxiety. (Manipulation) the psychoneurotic can produce a situation of "psychopathic fiction" wherever positive data concerning themselves and negative misinformation concerning others are created, wherever one's role as a region of a network of pawns or patrons are used, and one is trim into acceptive the psychopath's agenda.

Different shared traits could embrace pathological self-love, consistent irresponsibleness, autocracy, lack of sympathy, cruelty, meanness, impulsivity, a disposition to self-harm and addictions, social exploitation, hostility, anger and rage, vanity, emotional instability, rejection sensitivity, disposition, and also the use of primitive defense mechanisms that square measure pathological and self-loving. In line with her, these behaviors typically seem as unthinking manifestations of intense pain, and square measure typically not deliberate on be thought-about artful.

Manipulative behavior is intrinsic to narcissists; the World Health Organization uses manipulation to get power and self-loving provider.

SUBCONSCIOUS MIND

Our nous is responsive to the sources of our happiness; however, our acutely aware mind is usually unable to understand constant. To harness our full potential, our acutely aware and subconscious minds must add a bike.

The nous is the seat of our attitudes, emotions, and outlook on life. By harnessing the ability of the subconscious, {we can|we will|we area unit able to} concentrate on things that are necessary to America. Irrational fears hold America back from achieving our potential. Often, negative emotions like concern, loss of hope, loss of religion in the grouping, and God hold America back from being happy.

By harnessing the ability of the subconscious, we can management our mind and discretion.

Mind management techniques:

Here may be a bird's eye read of some common mind management techniques that may assist you to enhance your lives:

1. Mental image

By visualizing ourselves achieving success, we tend to train our minds to figure towards success. scan some sensible recommendations on the mental image in our post. Positive energy is often attracted.

However, insurmountable the goal could seem, by the positive visual image, we tend to attract smart luck! Sports psychiatrists use this method extensively to supply peak performances in athletes.

Khalil Kahlil Gibran has fenced in a couplet that states that no matter you single mindedly raise of the universe, the universe offers to you. this is often an affirmation of the ability of positive visual image that has additionally been reaffirmed by Rhonda Byrne within the recent standard film "The Secret."

2. Meditation

Meditation is one in all the oldest techniques of dominant the mind. By calming the mind and evacuation of all thoughts, we tend to enable peace and calm to flow into our minds. Meditation quiets disparate thoughts perpetually flitting through our mind and offers our subconscious its voice.

It is scientifically well-tried that the alpha waves made by the mind, a peak once meditation. Alpha waves enrich inventive and positive thinking. Meditation empowers the mind to concentrate on this and solely on what's necessary.

3. Mirror speak

Man is his supporter and worst enemy. Negative self-talk becomes a self-fulfilling prophecy. Invariably talking right down to down to} oneself are often a surefire way of being looked down upon by all.

If on the opposite hand, we tend to offer ourselves positive strokes and encourage ourselves, the mind feeds and focuses on what's accomplishable and works towards that goal.

4. Autosuggestion

Self-hypnosis and repetition of one mantra may be a technique that has been used with success by AA to free alcoholics from their dangerous alcohol dependency.

5. Writing down goals and continuous self-assessment

Writing down our goals offers them concrete kind. unceasingly reviewing goals and also the progress created towards achieving them allows you to create necessary the changes required. Reviewing the progress created additionally helps keep your purpose constant and spirits upbeat.

Read additional within the Power of goal setting.

Mind management techniques area unit effectively accustomed cure several ailments, in relieving acute pain, and in reducing stress. it's an amazing thanks to keeping positive and energetic in making attempt things.

Autosuggestion, for instance, maybe a mind management technique that's best accustomed get eliminate dangerous habits like smoking, drinking, and substance abuse.

It is rare that you simply might realize somebody or persons World Health Organization has achieved tremendous success in life while not a traditional state of mind. With all the same and done, the correct outlook is crucial to any pregnant action.

All the success stories touch to the employment of mind management tricks; can successively bear direct influence within the quality of one's life.

Starting and rising the subconscious power of the mind permits you to appreciate a rare chance to understand the sweetness and worth in life. Nothing in life is additional fulfilling and satisfying than to relax within the freedom and awareness that you simply square measure up to the speed of your mind and so connected along with your inner self. This suggests that achieving this association is by adopting some few, however effective mind management tricks. Some very little acknowledged mind power secrets square measure shrouded in uncommon secrecy.

There square measure 3 factors that square measure essential contributors to completely different areas of success in someone's life. These involve: using the mind power techniques to impact strategy.

Secondly, one ought to 'make a powerful commitment that has got to synchronize with a uniform set up of action.

Thirdly, is to implement very little acknowledged mind management tricks which can, within the end of the day, offer you the required boost in your space of implementation. The ensuing bumper action reveals itself as success in life. It suffices to list the advantages if one is committed to rise mind power. This goes to help in modeling daily routine exercises. Mind management tricks involve essential self-optical device focus, deep inner association additionally to complete self-management, whereas maintaining total awareness of your physical being.

Strict adherence to daily routine implementation of mind management tricks yields absolute clarity of things in the correct perspective. The realm of a person's subconscious self is analogous to giant info. every of these classified knowledge base strata springs from one's previous experiences.

These experiences would are gathered from completely different areas;

For example, learning nonheritable united grows through traditional life, teachings that you'll have received through either school rooms or the other supply.

The subconscious info acts to support one in realizing more success in future life. The standard yardstick is that after you unendingly and systematically work whereas implementing your mind management tricks, you'd be ready to clear and replace recent knowledge with the clear condition of mind.

Your mental warehouse is going to be recent with enough knowledge houses, able to accommodate recent data. It rests upon one to create a selection between recent inhibiting mental outlooks or prefer to take full advantage of the powerful mind management tricks that are certain to yield positive results. These tricks exist and square measure real within the gift day and time. Implementing the on top of mind ever-changing secrets is certain to supply endless success and a life filled with abundance.

It's a certain method of guaranteeing success with the liberty of mind that you have got perpetually desired. It's with double assurance, to state that the results aren't solely extraordinary however life-changing further. Attempt it and reap the advantages. You have got everything to realize.

Mind management Techniques to remember Isolation.

Physical isolation may be powerful; however, even once physical isolation is not possible or not sensible, manipulators can generally arrange to isolate you mentally. ...

Criticism. Criticism could also be used as an Associate in nursing isolation tool. ...

Social proof and peer pressure. ...

Fear of alienation. ...

Repetition. ...

Fatigue. ...

Forming a new identity.

Most people feel that mind management tricks are one thing sorcerous or associated with the globe of Voodoo. Well, actuality truth is that mind management tricks don't seem to be in the slightest degree associated with magic or the mental state world. As you all recognize, that mind is one in every of the foremost cogent tools which will modification all of your negative thinking to additional positive. It's believed that the human brain uses solely 100 percent of its original power throughout the lifetime. During this regard, mind management tricks may be wont to get additional success and to lift the brain level to ninetieth. Well, there are varied techniques to regulate the brain. All you wish to use your brain in the right direction! During this regard, such tricks offer you adequate facilitate. Here below, you'll get a number of the foremost effective mind dominant method:

Reverse scientific discipline: This can be one in every of the foremost ancient mind management technique.

Anyone will use it to draw outstanding results. During this technique, you've got to try and do one thing against that you just really need to try and do. Then, look forward to the person to be against you, and shortly, you'll notice that they're doing an identical issue that you just have anticipated. Reverse scientific discipline means that spoken language and doing one thing that's contrary to what you truly would like to happen, then looking forward to another person take this bait & oppose you, thus creating them to mention alternatively do what you precisely need to.

Reverse scientific discipline is the oldest form of mind management technique in a very book. You'll create use of it much in any reasonable scenario.

Be Positive largely, and it's been found that individuals react unenthusiastically after they notice rhythm words like "do not," "No," or "cannot." If you wish to draw folks towards you, then you wish to target optimistic points by victimization words that offer greater influence.

try and use words like "can" because it offers larger results and blessings. it is a true proven fact that folks forever wish to listen to positive words.

Call a Pal - If you need to influence somebody in keeping with your ways that, its higher to a decision a pal. Your friend will certainly provide you with smart support, and you'll simply accomplish your task. If you would like to steer someone to try and do one thing and conform to your thought, you'll decide your friend or someone World Health Organization is credible for supporting you. Folks are programmed for thinking that in style read is true opinion. So just in case if you wish a friend to hitch with you on the activity and that they are a touch hesitant, then you'll get another friend for the rear up.

Mind management tricks are a number of the foremost ethical and high-principled approach that you just will use. By victimization mind management tricks, you'll undoubtedly get legion blessings and edges.

Mind management tricks don't seem to be unethical & those who create use of them don't seem to be immoral. They recognize in a very approach their mind works & use this data to better of their profit.

One Sunday afternoon, a crowd of individuals visited watch an Oakland Raiders game. Throughout the second quarter, five different individuals came to the health facility feeling sick and expulsion. The doctor on workers found that almost all of them were sitting in one finish of the sports stadium. Suspecting sickness, he had security close up the concessions stands thereon facet of the building and had sports stadium officers build a public announcement over the loudspeakers instructing fans to not visit concession stands in this space because of the chance of sickness.

Before long, virtually two hundred individuals from that a part of the sports stadium came to the health facility feeling sick and showing alternative symptoms of sickness.

The workers began causing individuals over to the hospital for treatment once the doctor created a discovery. Whereas interviewing the initial five patients, he discovered that they had all consumed spoiled salad from a similar store across the road from the sports stadium. The food at the sports stadium was utterly safe.

Mind management mass sickness:

As presently as this new data was proclaimed, guess what happened to the opposite two hundred poisoned fans? They instantly got better! If truth be told, they went back to the sport before the half started! After they thought that they had been poisoned, their body began to exhibit the symptoms of sickness.

Isn't that amazing? Their thoughts alone made physical issues like expulsion and nausea!

This morning I used to be thinking tons about…well…thinking. A lot of specifics on the ability of our thoughts to influence our reality.

We've most detected the byword that claims, "As a person thinketh in his heart, so is he." (Proverbs 23:7) however, true is that statement? I feel it's implausibly true.

I do believe that we tend to can suppose a way nonetheless act another for a while; however, eventually, our thoughts can confirm our actions. It's inevitable. no one goes out and cheats on their married person while not having cheated in their mind for an amount of your time beforehand. no one commits a serious crime on a whim. There's an inspiration method 1st. A lot of we predict regarding one thing, a lot of probably it's to happen.

It is a blessing as a result of it conjointly works in our favor. roaring individuals don't seem ad-lib. they need to learn to focus their thoughts on success, productivity, goals, happiness, etc. A lot of them consider them; a lot of them begin to develop roaring habits.

A lot of roaring habits they need, the earlier they'll reach their goals for private success, no matter they will be.

Our character, and ultimately our destiny, come means down to} the way we tend to learn to focus our thoughts.

Law of the Harvest fingernail

Good thoughts eventually result in kickshaws. unhealthy thoughts about unhealthy things. Sow the seeds of positive thinking currently, and you may reap the harvest of success later.

Action Steps:

1. **Check your thoughts** – future time you've got a prospect from work, a spare moment, or once you're driving, be attentive to what you're pondering. Does one go straight to Facebook, consider a television program, or simply surface the radio? These aren't inherently unhealthy things. they're simply the natural place our brain

goes as a result of it needs very little effort. however, imagine the distinction if you spent longer pondering your semipermanent goals, the individuals you'll facilitate, a replacement talent you would like to find out, or a psychological feature story you're detected.

2. **Build a thought** to find three areas in your life wherever you'd wish to improve. Write them down so that they become goals rather than desires.

3. **Act on your set up once you have a flash within the day,** verify your list, and think about one thing you'll be able to do right then to enhance in one amongst those areas. If your set up was to lose five pounds, you'd do some jumping jacks. If you needed to assist a lot of individuals, seek somebody to go with or supply your facilitate to. {you can|you'll|you may} realize that performing on your positive thoughts will reinforce them, and you may begin pondering them a lot of typically. As we tend to aforementioned before, a lot of you think that

regarding them, a lot of they'll influence your actions, habits, and destiny.

Remember, you management your thoughts, and so you management your destiny.

DARK TRIAD PERSONALITIES

Managing "Dark" Personality Traits

Many people have complex personality traits and therefore they are very difficult to handle. They might have violent and aggressive behaviors but in a certain way, you can alter their behaviors. You can see the harmony and care in their personality as well. You can manage their behaviors with great management and skills.

Besides, some behaviors are very toxic and dangerous that you cannot manage them. These people can undermine their colleagues in a bad way. You cannot alter those behaviors in any way. Such people tend to damage all the teams.

Psychologists have identified and proposed three traits that make up the sinister-sounding "Dark Triad": narcissism, Machiavellianism, and psychopathy.

We are going to see what these three traits are and how they can affect the workplace.

What Is the Dark Triad?

The Dark Triad is a much unknown word to most of the people because it is one of the 'buzzwords'. This word is known in the world of psychology.

Narcissism: narcissism comes from the Greek myth of Narcissus, a hunter who fell in love with his reflection in a pool of water, and drowned. People are narcissistic who are selfish, boastful, arrogant, lacking in empathy, and hypersensitive to criticism.

The word derives from the renowned Italian politician and diplomat Niccolo Machiavelli of the 16th century. The major traits that associate with Machiavellianism are duplicity, manipulation, self-interest, and a lack of both emotion and morality.

Psychopathy: psychopathy refers to the traits including lack of empathy or remorse, antisocial behavior, and being manipulative and volatile. There is a distinction between a psychopath and psychopathic traits.

How to Identify Dark Triad Traits?

Traditionally, psychologists have identified Dark Triad traits by checking different traits one by one.

However, in 2010, Dr. Peter Jonason, then assistant professor of psychology at the University of Western Florida, and his co-author, Gregory Webster, assistant professor of psychology at the University of Florida, developed the "Dirty Dozen" rating scale, or a 12-item methodology, to measure Dark Triad traits.

Jonason and Webster's made people rate themselves according to the following questions:

- I tend to manipulate others to get my way.
- I have used deceit or lied to get my way.
- I have used flattery to get my way.
- I tend to exploit others towards my end.

- I tend to lack remorse.

- I tend to not be too concerned with morality or the morality of my actions.

- I tend to be callous or insensitive.

- I tend to be cynical.

- I tend to want others to admire me.

- I tend to want others to pay attention to me.

- I tend to seek prestige or status.

- I tend to expect special favors from others.

If a person has rated a higher score then it means that he or she has higher Dark Triad traits.

How to Manage People with Dark Triad Traits

If you find out someone likely to have Dark Triad traits then what to do?

This is one of the multifaceted areas and there are no easy answers. Experienced psychologists argued that behavior changes day to day and thus gradation of personality types also changes.

In other scenarios as a manager, you will need to address negative behaviors to maintain harmony and productivity within your team.

Coping With Anger

A person with psychopathic traits is likely to be more prone to anger and aggression. The usual signs of anger are easy to figure out for example a raised voice. There are also other ways of showing anger such as ignoring people. In this way, passive aggression occurs that is difficult to figure out and manage.

There are some strategies you can use when dealing with angry people. It is very necessary to make you secure first in front of an aggressive person. After some time you need to try to identify the cause of his rage   with Questioning   Techniques   and Active Listening.

Dealing With Bullying

There are occasions when anger comes out in the form of bullying. At an initial and simple level, it can be verbal abuse but gradually it becomes more threatening. Such persons start belittling others and spread unrealistic rumors.

If you spot bullying on your team, it's just as important to support the victim as it is to confront the bully and hold her accountable.

Spotting Manipulators

You need to go with a variety of options to impress others at your workplace. There are a lot of ways through which you can influence others. One way is to praise and encourage others at your workplace. But if someone has more Machiavellian tendencies, he could try to influence co-workers by selfishly manipulating them, perhaps through coercion or deception.

Manipulative people are often good at hiding their behavior or actions, but there are signs you can lookout. Those signs include someone who won't take an answer, who always excuses for hurtful behavior, or presents multi-faces to different people to fulfill the purposes. If you challenge a manipulative person then you need to have proof that how he is damaging your team.

Coping With Narcissism

The selfishness of narcissists can be a big headache because it can disturb the morale and ambiance of a workplace. People might not realize that they are affecting and damaging the whole team but you need to raise your voice against their actions.

Narcissists said to have a big ego and do whatever they can to grab the spotlight. He may demand credit for ideas, use "I" and "me" instead of "we," and can often dominate discussions or meetings.

People with big egos often don't expect to be challenged therefore you need to stand on the ground and meet their claims or demands with solid counter-arguments. It can also be useful to put them in a situation where they are dependent on colleagues' cooperation. This can increase respect and understanding.

Building the Skills You Need to Cope
It is very difficult to manage negative behaviors if you do not tend to manage them. if you don't feel confident in dealing with conflicts then you can face many difficulties in dealing with different types of people.

And there is a lot you can do to develop your ability to understand other people and recognize their emotional state and perspectives. You can boost your "people skills" by building empathy and emotional intelligence. You can better manage your own emotions with these skills, and having a greater understanding of other people can help you spot patterns of unwanted behavior before they become a threat to your team.

The Impact of Dark Triad Traits at Work

It's difficult to find anything positive in the impacts of Dark Triad traits at the workplace. In his 2013 paper, The Dark Side of Personality at Work, Dr. Seth Spain, assistant professor at Binghampton University School of Management in New York, said there was evidence of a "fairly robust relationship between Machiavellianism and unethical decision-making in organizations."

Research by Delroy Paulhus and Kevin Williams, psychologists at the University of British Columbia, argue that tendencies associated with narcissism, Machiavellianism, and psychopathy are entirely separate entities but they tend to overlap.

However, there is some evidence that initially narcissism can come across in relatively positive and desirable ways. A narcissist will often make an effort with his or her appearance and seem to be charming and friendly but constant self-obsession take away all the charm in just seconds.

Guarding Against the Subtle Influence of Dark Triad Individuals

In his 2013 book, Office Politics: How to Thrive in a World of Lying, Backstabbing and Dirty Tricks, psychologist Oliver James declares that Dark Triad tendencies can give someone a nefarious advantage in the workplace, in terms of career and progression. People with having Dark Triad tendencies can help people bully or manipulate their way to the top of an organization.

Patrick Fagan, an associate lecturer in consumer behavior at Goldsmiths, University of London, in the U.K., also suggests the dark traits can help individuals "get ahead," even if they don't "get along." Narcissists' high self-esteem may give them a high yearning for leadership, psychopathic people tend to focus on achievement without being too concerned at the effect their ambition might have on others, and Machiavellians can be very adept at portraying themselves in a good light.

Clive Boddy, Professor of Leadership and Organisation Behaviour at Middlesex University in the U.K., contends that Dark Triad traits can lead to the creation of "corporate psychopaths" with a diminished sense of corporate or collective responsibility. He argues such personality types are often more prevalent within sectors such as financial services and the civil service. (We can speculate that these behaviors may have played a key part in the catastrophe of the global financial crisis of 2004-08.)

These traits put the desires of one, "dark side" individual above the needs of the organization, the people within it, and those it serves, and this can destroy good organizations, particularly if this person is in a leadership role. So managers at all levels need to keep an eye out for Dark Triad behaviors, guard against them, and deal with them vigorously. (Where appropriate, this may involve removing people showing these behaviors from the organization.

FAQs ABOUT DARK PSYCHOLOGY

Q#1: Why call it "Dark" Psychology?

According to Michael Nuccitelli in 2006, *"Dark Psychology is… a study of the human condition as it relates to the psychological nature of people to prey upon others motivated by psychopathic, deviant, or psychopathological criminal drives. "All of humanity has the potentiality to victimize humans and other living creatures." Dark Psychology explores criminal, deviant, and cybercriminal minds."*

In other words, this branch of psychology studies the dark side of how people can misuse psychological tactics to get their way. People's intentions can be good or bad, but manipulative tactics are usually unethical and harmful for society as a whole because you are misusing someone's kindness and taking advantage of them.

Manipulation can also be conscious or unconscious, meaning some people do not even have a clue that they are manipulating the people around them. However, it does not change the fact that they are using dark psychological strategies that are disrespectful and bad. *Dark Psychology is not only the dark side of our moon, but the dark side of all moons combined."*

Q#2: Can manipulation only be used for bad?

Dark psychological tactics, such as manipulation and coercion, are considered to be bad. After all, no one likes to be manipulated.

The word 'manipulation' has a lot of negative connotations attached to it, whether it is in our professional lives or private, for example, people pushing us into doing something we do not want to do or the fact that when someone is manipulated, they are taken advantage of.

However, manipulation does not always have to be for the wrong reasons. Manipulation is of two types: Persuasion and coercion. Persuasion means trying to convince and motivate people to do something that wants to do, but her hesitant to. On the other hand, coercion is about making people do things that they do not want to do. So, technically, coercion is bad, and persuasion is good; however, that also varies from situation to situation, that is whether or not something someone wants to do is good for them, or whether what they do not want to do is bad for them.

Throughout times, people have had many different issues for which they needed professional help, now more than ever due to our fast-paced economic lifestyle. To cater to these issues, people go talk to therapists or psychologists for help, and these professionals use persuasive measures to help their patient improve their lifestyles. This is a form of manipulation, and persuasion is a dark psychological tactic. However, it is for the greater good and mental peace of the person.

Another way manipulation can be used to make your friends and family do good things that you know are good for society as a whole. One example of this can be that you know your family members have a bad habit of littering, or using a lot of plastic bottles and not recycling. You know that this is not sustainable and bad for the environment, and you want them to stop, but they won't listen to you. So, over some time, you start slowly manipulating them and guilt-tripping them until they are conditioned to do what is right and not litter. Technically, this is manipulation; however, your intentions were good, and you were doing it for a good reason, because you wanted your family to become better people, and you wanted to do something good for the environment.

Q#3: Where is the Dark Psychological Tactic of Coercion practically used?

In an ideal world, you will have asked someone for something, and they will do it for you. But this world is not ideal, and that is not how things work.

So, on a day to day routine, people often use dark psychological tactics to convince people of what they need to get things done. Besides, daily, however, these tactics are also used by professionals in different fields.

One of these fields is Sales and Marketing. Many salespeople become so focused on ensuring the customer buys something; they tend to start using dark tactics of manipulation to motivate and persuade them to buy the product of their company. Similarly, marketing companies use these tactics of persuasion to get people attracted to buying their products. Although debatable, some famous economists and philosophers have shown their strong disdain towards marketing and have classified it as highly unethical. They believe this to be so because they feel like marketing convinces people desperate to buy things that they do not need to survive, hence promoting consumerism. That, however, is a debate for another time.

Besides Sales and Marketing personnel, tactics of Dark Psychology are used by the Police as well, to solve cases and catch the bad guy, to ensure peace and prosperity within their jurisdictions. They use such strategies to coerce information out of witnesses and friends of their suspect and manipulate their suspects to also come clean. Besides this, these police officers and investigation agents are fully trained to read people's behaviors and body language, allowing them to get answers without the suspect having said anything at all.

CONCLUSION

It's important to be reminded that it's very easy to fall under the influence of dark psychological tactics, and also maybe even fall into bringing in use such tactics to get what we want. It is important to know the art of manipulation and persuasion to make sure no one uses it on you, but besides that, it is also important to know them to be consciously aware of not using them on other people, and to know when to stop yourself if you ever identify yourself to be using them. Even if you want to manipulate someone into doing good things, you should avoid it because then you are deceiving the person and breaking their trust. If you feel like your point of view is that of what a good person will do, then you should first and foremost try to convince them straightforwardly and honestly about how they should change certain aspects of their behavior, rather than being sycophantic about it and manipulating them into doing good.

Moreover, women very easily become victim to the tactics of dark psychology, so they should well aware of their surroundings, and whatever is going on around them, and what the men in their life are saying and doing, and they should observe the behavior of males in general to understand the baseline behavior and how and when they are deviating from it.

Dark psychology is a very vast and informative field, as it caters to the negativities and evil side of humanity, which not many other fields do. It helps us to understand why men and women are manipulating their friends, family, coworkers, and whatnot. However, as mentioned before, as well, one should never use such tactics, even if the intention is good. The only time using such methods is to be considered ethical is when there is a "win-win" situation for both you and the person on whom you are using these tactics.

For this, you must be honest with yourself into analyzing the situation and TRULY believe that what you are doing is beneficial for the other person as well. If it is solely for your benefit, then you can quite easily fall into and become addicted to carrying out wrong and unethical practices.